FAITH

Devdutt Pattanaik writes, illustrates and lectures on the relevance of mythology in modern times. He has, since 1996, written over fifty books and 1000 columns on how stories, symbols and rituals construct the subjective truth (myths) of ancient and modern cultures around the world. His books include *7 Secrets of Hindu Calendar Art* (Westland), *Myth=Mithya: A Handbook of Hindu Mythology* (Penguin Random House), *Jaya: An Illustrated Retelling of the Mahabharata* (Penguin Random House), *Sita: An Illustrated Retelling of the Ramayana* (Penguin Random House), *Olympus: An Indian Retelling of the Greek Myths* (Penguin Random House), *Business Sutra: A Very Indian Approach to Management* (Aleph Book Company), *My Gita* (Rupa Publications) and the Devlok with Devdutt Pattanaik series (Penguin Random House). To know more, visit devdutt.com.

By the same author

Shiva to Shankara: Giving Form to the Formless
Culture: 50 Insights from Mythology
Leader: 50 Insights from Mythology

FAITH

40 INSIGHTS INTO HINDUISM

Devdutt Pattanaik

Illustrations by the author

Harper
Collins

First published in hardback in India by
HarperCollins *Publishers* in 2019
A-75, Sector 57, Noida, Uttar Pradesh 201301, India
www.harpercollins.co.in

2 4 6 8 10 9 7 5 3 1

Text and illustrations copyright © Devdutt Pattanaik 2019
An earlier version of the articles that comprise this book
previously appeared in DailyO.in

P-ISBN: 978-93-5302-596-0
E-ISBN: 978-93-5302-597-7

Typeset in Garamond by Special Effects Graphics Design Co., Mumbai

Printed and bound at
Thomson Press (India) Ltd

MIX
Paper
FSC   FSC® C010615

This book is produced from independently certified FSC® paper
to ensure responsible forest management.

Contents

Customs

Scriptures

History

Why this book

There are two reasons for this book. One relates to the past, the other to the future.

First, the reason related to the past: Many Hindus find it difficult to explain the origins, and hence the logic, of Hindu customs and beliefs, even to their own children. Not surprising, as it is not as organized a religion as Islam or Christianity. It becomes even more difficult when any questions about Hinduism are received with hostility. Matters become worse when the answers are dismissed, and Hindus are branded as defensive, apologetic, even chauvinistic. It does not help that the global village functions using Western 'humanistic' or 'social justice' frameworks that owe their origin to Western religions (where God is judge on Judgement Day) despite claiming to be secular. That is why they are at dissonance with Eastern thought, especially Hinduism (where God is no judge and there is no concept of Judgement Day). Hence this book.

Second, the reason related to the future: Hindus need to outgrow their tendency to locate 'pure' Hinduism to a time, or to a geography, or to a scripture. This usually results in fundamentalism. In a global village, as people migrate to different lands and mingle with different people, we need to view Hinduism with a more forward-looking gaze, in terms of transformation: fruits more than roots. Hinduism practiced in a village in India cannot be the same as that practiced in an Indian city, or in an American, European, Australian, African or Chinese neighbourhood. Reframing and realignment are needed to make it relevant to contemporary space and time. We must remember how Hindu sages who wrote the dharma-shastras always advised adapting rules to time (kala), place (sthana) and people (patra). The idea of one truth that is finite, absolute, universal and equally relevant to all is not a Hindu idea. Empathy for diversity, of gods and of truths and of interpretations, is the key to gaining insight into Hinduism.

Faith answers questions about Hinduism with love and dignity. It provides as many facts as possible, but is ultimately based on my personal understanding, years of study and comparing Hindu with world mythology. Mythology reveals cultural truths, encoded in stories, symbols and rituals. As you go through the book keep in mind that nature is diverse, culture is dynamic, and our mind that transmits, and receives ideas, has its limitations. Don't seek perfection. Don't seek destination. Seek tendencies, drifts and directions, because:

Within infinite myths lies an eternal truth
Who sees it all?
Varuna has but a thousand eyes
Indra, a hundred
You and I, only two.

Devdutt Pattanaik

Belief

1

What are Vedic values, or the Indian ethos of Hindus?

Although words like Vedic and Hindu are used interchangeably, technically speaking, the Vedic period is pre-Buddhist and over 3000 years old while Hinduism as we know it today took concrete shape around 2000 years ago when the Ramayana, Mahabharata and Puranas reached their final forms, along with the dharma-shastras, artha-shastras, kama-shastras and moksha-shastras. Bhakti peaked only 1000 years ago. Throughout, however, there were some ideas that were consistent. But can we call these ideas 'values'?

The concept of universal values, which we find in the corporate world too, comes to us from Abrahamic mythology, where the God of Abraham puts down a set of rules and values (commandments) about how humans are supposed to conduct their lives. These rules and values are transmitted by messengers known as prophets. They are meant for all humans, for Abrahamic mythology believes everyone is equal before God and hence his rules and values apply equally to all. However, few people agree on what the correct set of rules and values are. This disagreement leads to fights between Jews, Muslims and Christians. They don't even agree if the day of rest should be Saturday, Friday or Sunday.

Secular nation states simply replace God with 'We, the People' or the 'State' and use the same Abrahamic model of governance based on rules/values that everyone is supposed to follow.

The Vedic worldview is very different. It is based not on rules or values, rather on the evolution of the mind. Here, nature (prakriti) came first, before culture (sanskriti). It functions as per the 'law of jungle' where might is right, only the fit survive, and so driven by hunger and fear animals establish food chains, pecking orders and territories. Humans beings are animals with imagination. We have the ability to not subscribe to this jungle way. We can help the helpless. We can provide resources to help the unfit survive. We don't have to form packs, or herds. We don't have to dominate others or be territorial. This is dharma. When we don't do that, when we are not in line with our potential, we are following adharma. Humans have the ability to think of others (para-atma) and so can reach the infinite divine (param-atma) beyond the self (jiva-atma). When we do that, we are in line with our potential. We are evolving.

As we study the transformation of Hinduism over 3000 years, from Vedic to Puranic times, we notice an obsession with concepts such as infinity (ananta), diversity (aneka), and impermanence (anitya). This establishes a worldview that is the very opposite of Abrahamic thought which seeks to 'fix' the world by rules and values. In the Hindu world everyone's context is different. Everyone's needs, wants, hungers and fears are different. All values and rules change with space (sthana), time (kala) and people (patra). Since Abrahamic mythology values equality, it values homogeneity over heterogeneity. Hindu mythology values diversity, and so appreciates that there cannot be one set of rules/values in a plural world. Also Hindu mythology factors in dynamism – the idea that everything changes over time.

That is why in the Ramayana we have a rule-following hero (Ram) and a rule-breaking villain (Ravana), and in the Mahabharata we have a rule-breaking hero (Krishna) and a rule-following villain (Duryodhana). The problem is not rules/values. The problem is not obedience or disobedience. The problem is the animal within that refuses to rise to its human potential of empathy.

In the Vedic worldview, the focus is not on rules and values and obedience and punishment. The focus is on dharma, on engaging with others with awareness and working towards reducing our own hunger and fear. High hunger and fear nourish ego (aham), and takes us away from divinity (atma). When humans seek to dominate and control other people for self-aggrandizement, it is aham at work. When we enable people to empathize with each other, and seek to delight, rather than defeat and control others, then atma is at work. Rules and values are just hygiene.

In the end, the question becomes: does one work only for self (jiva-atma) or is one concerned about the other (para-atma)? Ram and Krishna work for others, Ravana and Duryodhana work for the self. We are all in between, hopefully moving towards dharma and atma (Ram/Krishna).

We can say that while the Abrahamic religions of the world and secular society value policies to improve the world, Hinduism values psychological evolution, and empathy instead. This can be exasperating to the impatient. But then what is the hurry? The world is limitless and this is but one of our many lives, as per Hinduism.

Faith: 40 Insights into Hinduism

2

How did the world come into being according to Hinduism?

There is no one story in Hinduism of how the world came into being. But it is in striking contrast to the story of Genesis found in the Bible, where God creates the world out of nothingness, as well as to the Big Bang theory of science, that values matter over mind.

In Abrahamic mythology, the world has a definite beginning and a definite end, like a segment, essentially. In Hinduism, the world is like a line, endless, and even repetitive, with no clear beginning or end. This difference in the notion of time, explains the difference in the Creation myths. While there is Genesis in Jewish, Christian and Islamic traditions, there isn't one in Hinduism.

Hinduism – like Buddhism and Jainism – views the world as eternal, going through phases of creation and destruction.

Thus, 'beginning' refers to the beginning of a phase, not the world itself. Because Hinduism is plural in nature, with a vast collection of customs and beliefs of numerous communities that have come into being, over many periods of history, there is no single story of creation.

In Hinduism, when we speak of 'creation', we should clarify what we are speaking of – the birth of matter, of consciousness, of living creatures, or of culture. It is never clear as a whole set of different ideas are expressed in various Vedic and Puranic texts.

There are many stories of how the world came into being, some from the Vedas, some from the Brahmanas, some from the Puranas; some are philosophical tales based on concepts, and others are narratives based on characters. One can sense something common in all of them, but there is a great deal of variation.

In early Vedic hymns, the world is an organism (purusha) created by the sacrifice of the primal being. Culture is also an organism, created by the union of four types of people: the knowledge-keepers (Brahmin) who constitute the organism's head, the land-controllers (Kshatriya) who constitute the arms, the market-controllers (Vaishya) who constitute the trunk, and service-providers (Shudra) who constitute the feet. Thus creation involves breaking apart and coming together.

Later Puranic traditions speak of Brahma as the creator. Here, the reference is to the creation of life (sentient beings) not the world (matter). They also refer to human culture, not nature. Culture goes through four phases – childhood (Krita), youth (Treta), maturity (Dvapara) and old age (Kali) – before dying (Pralaya) after which there is rebirth. The death is imagined as a flood, and the only thing that survives is the first human, Manu, and the Vedas, saved by Vishnu. This is a recurring event.

Brahma is also called Prajapati, the father of all living creatures. And so, from his mind are created 'mind-born' sons, the sages – a reference to asexual reproduction. After this come sons who marry women and produce children. According to the Puranas, Rishi Kashyapa, a son of Brahma, marries many women who give birth to different kinds of creatures. Timi gives birth to fishes, Kadru to snakes and Vinata to birds. But it is never clear where the women come from: are they from Brahma's body or elsewhere? Brahma and all male forms seem like metaphors for the mind that is planted in matter (represented as women) to create embodied life.

This union of a male and female form, of mind and matter, has been a recurring theme in the Puranic tradition, especially after the rise of Tantra. Shiva cannot create the world without Shakti; without her, he starves. This world of Shiva and Shakti is nature. In the Gita, this duality is denied. Krishna claims that he is source of life, that he has two 'wombs' (yoni), which are mind and matter. Some people prefer using the word 'consciousness' instead of 'mind'.

What comes first – mind or matter? In the old Vedic hymns, the most famous 'creation' hymn doubts if this question can ever be answered. This scepticism is found in Upanishads too, although many attempts are made to answer the question.

Later, in the Tantras, we are told that matter came first as the Goddess, and from her came the mind, taking three male forms: Brahma, the priest; Vishnu, the king; Shiva, the ascetic. Brahma sought control of the Goddess, and was beheaded. Shiva sought to reject the Goddess and was enchanted and turned into her husband. Vishnu became the caretaker as well as the beloved of the Goddess. Brahma's desire to control the Goddess is given as the reason why he is not worshipped.

However, in the Puranas, the mind comes first. The world comes into being when Vishnu awakens and from his navel rises a lotus in which sits Brahma. Alone and afraid, unaware of his origins, he creates various living creatures from his mind. And assumes he is the creator – another reason why he is not worshipped.

Vishnu worshippers, who became dominant 1000 years ago, insisted that the world comes into being when Vishnu awakens and ceases to be when Vishnu sleeps. It is he who rescues the world from the bottom of the sea, and enables the churning of the ocean of milk so that Lakshmi can emerge.

Shiva worshippers rejected this idea. They tell the story of the pillar of fire, the embodiment of the consciousness, that has no beginning or end, whose tip Brahma could not find when he took the form of a swan, and whose base Vishnu could not find when he took the form of a boar. Thus, Shiva is the infinite origin around which all finite forms take shape.

The different modes in which one can look at the basis of creation allow us to indulge and celebrate the myriad possibilities of existence. They do not restrict a worldview to just one. Herein, one finds, yet again, the dynamic diversity of Hinduism.

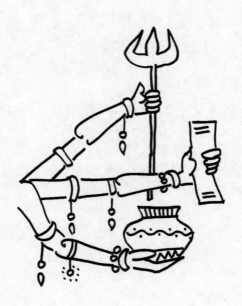

3

Why do many non-Hindus refer to Hinduism as mythology, not religion?

 Mythology basically denotes the beliefs of a people communicated through stories, symbols and rituals. In the tenth century, a worldview based on one God (monotheism) was religion, while that based on many gods (polytheism) was mythology. Today all worldviews, with one God or many gods or no God, are mythologies.

Hinduism accommodates many beliefs: no God (atheism), many gods (polytheism), one God (monotheism), Goddess, and a combination of these. This becomes a source of confusion for most people in the West for whom religion is the belief in one God, one book and one way of life. In other words, the West tends to use Christianity, Islam and Judaism as global benchmarks of religion. The West's love for Buddhism

cf. Gauri's remarks

stems from the fact that it can be traced to a single founder, Gautama Buddha.

Those who are uncomfortable with mythology are essentially people who believe in one truth: THE truth. They can be classified into two groups: those who follow monotheistic religions like Judaism, Christianity and Islam, and those who believe that humans are rational and function according to scientific principles. For this second group of people, truth is objective, factual and measurable, not subjective, faith-based, and beyond the scope of measurement.

Until the scientific revolution in the sixteenth century, Europe was controlled by the Christian church which assumed it alone knew the truth, and persecuted Jews and Muslims, who also claimed to know the truth. When in fact all Christians, like Jewish and Muslim people, believed in the God of Abraham, and simply disagreed on God's messenger (Moses, or Jesus, or Muhammad) and his message (Torah, Gospel, Quran). Naturally, they saw Hindus, when they encountered them, as heathens and pagans who had yet to discover the God of Abraham.

Since the advent of scientific religion, faith in God itself is seen as mythology, as God is not a measurable, or verifiable, concept. This has peaked since the Second World War, when the God of Abraham was seen as failing humanity. Hence, increasingly, young educated people are renouncing religion and embracing science, rationality and atheism. This is making the religious folk very angry and insecure. Monotheists who rejected Hinduism as mythology, are discovering that they themselves are in myth, for God is not a measurable scientific concept. So, they reject scientific ideas like evolution (a series of biochemical events resulted in life), and insist on religious ideas like creationism (God created the world). America has become a battleground between Christians and these rational-atheists. Europe remains avowedly less religious but is confused on how to deal with Muslim refugees, who want the opportunities of the West, created by science, but cling to their version of God and value that message over that of a democratic state.

Thus, in America and Europe, religion and secular nation-states are at loggerheads. There is internal fighting with the Church, and external fighting with the Muslims. The Right is seen as pro-Christian and anti-rationality and anti-Muslim. The Left claims to be rational, but in its hatred for the Christian Jewish lobby, often sides with the Muslim lobby, claiming its concern is humanitarian, and ignoring Islamic radicalization. What is common is that every side believes they have exclusive access to THE truth, hence the obsession with debates and the virulent argument to get their views across. Few notice that rules of material science cannot be applied to social sciences because it involves factoring human imagination that defies measurement.

Hinduism has always valued imagination. Those who wish to turn it into a religion, try to force Hinduism into an Abrahamic template of one God, one messenger, one rule book, and one way of life. They end up simply creating yet another version of Hinduism.

Hinduism has always made room for multiple truths and sees truths quantitatively (limited/limitless) and not qualitatively (true/false). In effect, there is your truth and my truth, and only God knows the Truth. Your truth and my truth may be based on monotheism, polytheism or atheism, but both are limited with the scope to expand. Only God's truth is infinite and limitless. Who is God? Who knows? Since the human mind is finite while God is infinite, reason or measurement cannot be used to discover God. Hinduism, then, depending on perspective, can be termed as a mythology, or a religion, or both, or neither. Like all faiths and ideologies, it is a way of looking at the world, a worldview.

4

Can I be a Hindu and still an atheist?

 One cannot define Hinduism. Therefore, the simple answer to the question is: yes, you can be a Hindu and still be an atheist. Those who try to define and standardize Hinduism may completely disagree and insist Hinduism is theist. The problem then lies with how we define God.

When people around the world talk of religion, they refer mostly to Judaism, Christianity and Islam. When they use the word 'God' (singular, capitalized, masculine), they are, probably, referring to the God of Abraham, who informs Judaism, Christianity and Islam. This is God who is outside humanity, and outside creation, who creates the world and humanity, loves humanity, and gives instructions through prophets on how humans should live. This God has cast down humanity to the world for breaking his rules in the perfect Eden. He gives humans one chance to live, to prove their love for him. In Judaic mythology, he punishes those who do not listen to him. In Christian mythology, he sacrifices his own son, Jesus, for the sins of humanity. In Islamic mythology, he appoints Muhammad as the last of his prophets. The most important aspect of these dominant religions is the idea of the 'covenant' or contract with God, expressed through the rite of baptism in Christianity, and circumcision in Judaism and Islam. The contract demands rejecting false gods, and idolatry.

But when Hindus use the word 'God', it is not the God of Abraham. They are referring to something that is both inside organisms and outside. God in Hinduism can be with or without form, masculine or feminine, singular or plural, and limitless or limited by space and time. Limitless Divine is spelt with capitalization; limited divine is spelt without capitalization. Thus, we can have Gods and Goddesses as well as gods and goddesses. All are manifestations of the Divine. There is no concept of Devil. Most importantly, Hinduism is rooted in the idea of rebirth (karma). There is no concept of Eden, Original Sin, commandments or one life. The Hindu idea of God does not speak so much about rejecting false gods as it does about understanding infinite forms of God.

Hindu mythology assumes the material world to be self-sustaining and self-created, but dependent on a spiritual principle (atma), non-material, described variously as consciousness, soul, awareness, essentially non-measurable. This is explained in various ways, using different frameworks, in the Vedanta, Tantra, Puranas and Agamas. Details vary in different schools of thought, across sects and traditions, known as sampradayas and paramparas. Details have changed over history (Hinduism in pre-Buddhist era is different from colonial era), and they vary over geography (Hinduism in Odia traditions is very different from Rajasthani ones).

God in Hinduism is often explained by modern gurus as cosmic consciousness (param-atma) who is in every living creature (jiva-atma). Vishnu and Shiva and Devi, as well as Ganesha and Kartikeya are limitless forms of param-atma, whereas Ram, Krishna and Ganga, are limited forms of param-atma as they are located on earth and so experience mortality. However, things are not so simple: Ram and Krishna can be God and god simultaneously; Hanuman transforms from god to God in the Ramayana. Trees, animals, rocks and even sages, can be seen as gods, or Gods. Gods take mortal forms to enable the god within us to become God, move from the world of limitations to the world of limitlessness. Limited forms entrap us in the world of ego, hunger, fear and death. The limitless liberates us, we merge with the cosmic, and are eternally tranquil.

It is significant to note that Buddhism and Jainism, which also believe in rebirth, and have many overlapping concepts, have no concept of God who created the world and rewards or punishes humanity for its actions. Buddhism rejects the idea of atma. Jains reject the concept of param-atma, but not jiva-atma. Both value teachers, sages who have attained infinite wisdom (kaivalya), hence called bhagavan.

In Hinduism, 'bhagavan' and 'ishwar' are terms used for the limitless divine. The difference is that bhagavan engages with the material world more than ishwar who is distant and aloof. Vishnu is often called bhagavan and Shiva is often called ishwar. But like everything Hindu, these definitions and nomenclatures are relatively fluid.

What it comes down to is this: Hinduism is about discovering God-ness in ourselves, by reflecting on the God outside us, hearing his stories and venerating his, or her, images, as against believing in an external all-powerful God. One can say that a Hindu theist is subscribing to the Hindu *definition* of God while a Hindu atheist is rejecting the Abrahamic *definition* of God.

Faith: 40 Insights into Hinduism

5

Who is a guru?

In the Advayataraka Upanishad, a guru is someone who takes one from darkness (gu) to light (ru). However, different people use the word 'guru', in different contexts to refer to different kinds of people. In popular parlance, it is used casually to mean teachers (adhyapak), coaches (acharya), mystics, occultists and magicians (jogi, siddha, tantrik), priests (purohit), monks (bhikshu, sanyasi, sadhu, muni), spiritual acolytes (arhat, tapasvee, yogi) and experts (shastri, pandit, gyani).

The Vedas do not refer to gurus as much as seers (rishi) who observe the world and transmit their knowledge and insights via hymns (mantra) to their students. In the Upanishads we find students such as Yagnavalkya fighting with teachers such as Vaisampayana, and rishis such as Ashtavakra having conversations kings such as Janaka to discover the truth.

There is no concept of a guru as a fountainhead of knowledge on whom one must be dependent. Here, the autonomy and independence of students matter.

In the Ramayana, Vasistha and Vishwamitra, who are called teachers (acharya), pass on a vast array of knowledge and skills to Ram. In the Mahabharata, Kripa and Drona pass on military skills and knowledge to the Pandavas and Kauravas. They are all referred to as gurus in common parlance.

In the Puranas, we are told, without Brihaspati, the devas cannot win a war, and without Shukra, the asuras cannot resurrect the dead. They seem like magicians and occultists. What kind of gurus were they?

In the Bhagavata Purana, Krishna tells Uddhava of the twenty-four gurus of the detached ascetic (avadhut). Here he includes various elements, plants, animals and life-experiences that give the ascetic awareness. Thus, a guru becomes one who rouses insight. But in the Skanda Purana, we find Shiva telling Parvati in the Guru Gita that without a guru, it is impossible for a person to understand the Vedas, or gain enlightenment. The Bhagavata Purana looks at a guru as one who acknowledges and enables human *independence*; the Skanda Purana looks at a guru as one on who facilitates human *dependence*.

In many ways, 2500 years ago, Buddha began as a guru who wanted his students to be independent. But over centuries, we see how his students increasingly became dependent. Buddha democratized spiritual practice, and entry into which had nothing to do with one's caste (jati). Anyone could join by simply declaring submission (sharanam) to the potential of awakening (buddha), the Buddhist doctrine (Dhamma) and the Buddhist community (sangha). But, as learnt from the Buddhist scriptures (pitaka), as more people joined, more rules, more quarrels and more splits began to manifest. Eventually, in Mahayana Buddhism especially, there came to be those who saw Buddha less as a philosopher or teacher, and more as a God-like figure to be worshipped, one who performed miracles, and who could solve mundane earthly problems if one truly had faith in him.

In the history of Christianity also we find such transformations. Jesus, who is first a preacher, distinguishes himself from being a messenger of God by calling himself the son of God, and eventually his followers are convinced he is God on earth. Even his mother becomes venerable, worthy of adoration, though not quite Goddess. Likewise, in Islam, importance is given not just to God's words as revealed in the Quran but also to the habits of Muhammad, declared to be the last and final prophet by his followers, as documented in the Hadith.

In Jainism there is a clear demarcation between the Tirthankara (the guru of gurus) and the regular monks and nuns who teach (shramana), and the lay followers who listen to the teachers (shravaka). The teachers are not allowed to stay anywhere for more than a day, except during the rainy season. They are expected to keep fasting and keep moving and shunning all material comforts, even clothes.

As Buddhism waned in India, in the past 1000 years, many spiritual scholars of Hinduism such as Ramanuja, Madhva, Vallabha and Basava established various monastic orders (matha), sects (sampradaya), traditions (parampara) and gymnasiums (akhara), many attached to temple complexes, complete with rules, temples and institutions, much like the Buddhist sangha. They were skilled administrators. They were patronized by kings such as those of Vijayanagar and the Nayaks of Tanjore. Many of these were monastic institutions established to safeguard Hindu dharma from Turuku dharma, a new way of life based on Islam, brought into India from the northwest about 800 years ago. Under the influence of Islam, the word 'guru' started being used as a synonym for 'paigambar' (God's messenger), an Abrahamic concept, which is very different from the Hindu concept of a detached hermit (digambar, shramana, gosain) who seeks the truth.

As the bhakti movement spread from the south and became popular in north India 500 years ago, gurus, pirs and sants established many camps (dera) in the countryside. Today these have become large institutions. Sikhism, for example, has become a religion. It evolved out of ten gurus, complete with a holy book filled with devotional hymns. Over time, it has divided the spiritual pursuit (piri) from material rules (miri), recognizing the tension between the other-worldly sage (pir) and the worldly governor (amir), much like the Vedic tension between seers (rishi) and kings (raja) that often led to confrontation, as narrated in the story of Parashurama.

Today, the word 'guru' is used globally for Indian spiritual leaders who insist they are detached from all things worldly but relish the wealth and power bestowed upon them by their *dependent* followers who typically express their submissiveness and humility, hence lack of ego, by addressing the leader as 'master' (swami, nath) or 'lord' (maharaj). Eventually the 'guru' becomes more important than God, as it happened in Buddhism. Guru becomes a territory who must be protected as bees protect the queen bee, for without the queen bee the security and nourishment provided by the beehive is gone. This mindset is reflected in the Guru Gita that states that a guru is equal to or greater than one's father, mother, the gods even.

In New Age gurudoms around the world, we find followers who function much like clans and tribes. Gurus cater to different social classes, some for the rich English-speaking city folk and the diaspora, and others for the non-English-speaking village folk, who feel disenchanted with the state and with organized religion. As their sex scandals emerge, and we find them increasingly serving the vote banks of politicians, in exchange for favours that help them establish vast 'spiritual' conglomerates selling 'spiritual' products, services and ideas, one is forced to wonder who is a real guru?

The answer ultimately depends on the follower. For some, a guru acts as a 'spiritual balm' and a never-ending fountain of 'positive energy' who solves problems magically. They allow the guru to infantilize themselves, accept no responsibility and stay emotionally dependent. For others, a guru is one with gravitas, who, dispelling blindness, provokes insight, enables independence and moves on like a wandering avadhut.

6

Can rakshasas or asuras be called the Hindu devil?

 e often assume that all religions are the same and every mythology must have a devil. However, there is no devil in Hinduism. We wrongly believe that 'shaitan' is the Hindi word for devil – it is an Urdu word rooted in Persian thought.

Hindu mythology does not have the concept of the devil because Hinduism does not have the concept of evil, and it does not have the concept of evil because it is based on the idea of rebirth and karma. The concept of evil, and its embodiment, the devil (or shaitan), plays a significant part in Christian and Islamic mythology, as they are based on the idea of one life, followed by an eternal afterlife.

Evil is a concept used by religious folk in the West to explain negative events that have no root cause. God is good and kind and so he cannot be the source of hurricanes and tornadoes, and murders and rape. So, these negative events are attributed to the devil who spreads evil. Of course, people argue, if God is all powerful why does he not defeat the devil and end all negative events. To this, the priests who have appointed themselves as God's defence lawyers say: We are suffering for the evil decisions made by humans who have succumbed to the devil's temptations. God had given humans the freedom to choose between himself and the devil, between good and evil.

Such ideas, however, are alien to Hinduism, Buddhism and Jainism, where all events are the outcome of karma. Every action is karma. Every reaction is karma. Every cause is karma. Every consequence is karma. We live in a web of karma. We have control over our karma, but not on karma generated by others. And so, bad things happen to good people and good things happen to bad people. Good and bad are human judgements, based on how we interpret the world. There is no good or bad in the world itself; it's an outcome of human understanding.

People prefer to divide the world into binaries of good and bad, right and wrong. But the wise see the bigger picture, and hold no one responsible for good or bad events. They need neither God nor the devil. Every event, even the inexplicable, irrational ones, has a cause. There is no God or devil out there causing it. God, in Hinduism, is our ability to be wise, to look beyond good and evil.

So, who are the asuras and rakshasas? How does one describe Andhaka, who is killed by Shiva, or Kansa, who is killed by Krishna, or Ravana, who is killed by Ram, or Mahisha, who is killed by Durga? Is asura a synonym for rakshasa? Or are they different? For this we must go back to the basics of Hindu mythology.

The Puranas say that all creatures are born of Brahma. From Brahma come various rishis and prajapatis who father different kinds of living creatures. Kashyapa, son of Brahma, has many wives such as Aditi, Diti and Danu, who give birth to the adityas, daityas and danavas respectively. Though born of the same father, the adityas and daityas are always quarrelling. English writers called adityas the gods of Hinduism and daityas the demons of Hinduism. Daityas and danavas are clubbed together as asuras. Devas were deemed good and asuras bad. But things are not so simple.

Diti was about to give birth to a child greater than Indra, leader of the adityas. Indra cut the embryo into eleven parts. Each part started to cry. Indra said, 'Don't cry,' and so they called themselves maruttas, the children who don't cry. They were also called rudras, the howlers. They became followers of Indra, and friends of the adityas. Thus, the thirty-three 'devas' or gods of Vedic-Hindu mythology comprised twelve adityas and eleven maruttas as well as eight vasus and two ashwins, not all born of the same mother, but everyone traced to the same father, Kashyapa. Enemies of the devas, also born of Kashyapa, were called asuras. Their battle was vertical, between earth and sky, with asuras inhabiting the realm under the earth (patala) and devas occupying the glittering realm beyond the sky (swarga).

Lakshmi is often called patala-nivasini (resident of the nether regions) as all wealth comes from under the earth. She is called Paulomi (daughter of the asura-king Puloman) which makes her asura-putri (daughter of asuras), who rises from below to become deva-patni (bride of the gods).

Asuras are sometimes like tree spirits who are killed. Like trees they have the power to regenerate as their guru, Shukra, possesses sanjivani vidya. Hence, we find gods kills asuras during harvest festivals such as Diwali and Dussehra: Krishna kills Narakasura, Durga kills Mahishasura, Vishnu overpowers Bali. They come back year after year, their death providing nourishment to humanity.

Rakshasas are not asuras. They descended from another son of Brahma – Pulatsya. From Pulatsya came Vishrava, from whom came the rakshasas and the yakshas, who were led by Ravana and Kubera respectively, according to the Ramayana. Just as the devas fought asuras, the rakshasas fought yakshas. Rakshasas lived in the south while yakshas moved north. Rakshasas also fought rishis. Rishis clubbed the rakshasas with asuras. Hence, in the Mahabharata, the various forest dwellers who oppose the Pandavas and the Vedic lifestyle – Baka, Hidimba, Jata, Kirmira – are all called asuras. The Vedic lifestyle was based on yagna, that is exchange, you give to receive, while the rakshasas' lifestyle was based on either grabbing or sharing, suggesting an old tribal order. In fact, rakshasas are described as guardians (rakshak) of the forest. Thus, the battle here suggests conflict between rishis, who preferred agriculture and trade, and rakshasas, who preferred old hunter–gatherer ways. Rakshasas are in conflict with humans and sages. Ram kills Ravana and his brothers and his sons. They are seen to follow matsya nyaya, or the fish law, which is law of the jungle: might is right. Ram and the rishis follow the way of dharma, where the mighty must protect the weak. The battle between rakshasas and rishis is horizontal on earth, between settled village communities and nomadic tribals. This is different from the vertical orientation of the battles between the devas who live in the sky and asuras who live under the earth.

In the list of different types of marriage, deva-marriage is when the father gives his daughter to a man who proves his worthiness by serving the father; asura-marriage is where a man buys a wife; and a rakshasa-marriage is one where a man abducts a wife. Thus, we see asuras linked to wealth and rakshasas to force.

Christian missionaries and European orientalists were eager to show that Hinduism was either like Greek or Norse mythology (drawing parallels between asuras and rakshasas and Titans or anti-gods or old gods) or like Christian mythology (aligning asuras and rakshasas with the devil). Indians educated in English got confused and started using rakshasas and asuras interchangeably. Both were 'demons'. Both were manifestations of the devil.

Contrarians and social activists went out of their way with no data to speculate wildly and prove these 'demons' were wronged, subaltern people, dark Dravidians and tribals overpowered by white Aryans. They used simplistic racial arguments and pointed to look at the black/green colour of Mahisha. They ignore that Ram and Krishna are portrayed as dark while Ravana (a rakshasa) and Prahalada (an asura) are painted as fair.

Hinduism saw asuras and rakshasas as different types of beings, born of Kashyapa and Pulatsya, one living under the earth, and one living in forests. Devas had amrita (nectar of immortality) while asuras had sanjivani vidya (knowledge of resurrection). Both were equally powerful. Devas were powerful in summer, asuras in winter. Rakshasas were seen as barbarians by some as they opposed the Vedic way. Yet the king of rakshasas in the Ramayana is a Vedic scholar, who is associated in later scriptures with Tantra, Shaivism and Tantrism. We learn of good rakshasas like Vibhishan, who adores Ram, just as we learn of good asuras like Prahalada, who adore Vishnu.

Words like 'evil' and 'devil' have no meaning in a worldview that deals with rebirth. Therefore, these words have no significance in Hinduism, Buddhism or Jainism. Asuras and rakshasas are powerful, eternal forces that we may not like but must co-exist with. We live in a web of multiple forces, some that help us and some that harm us. The forces themselves are neither negative or positive. It's our relationship with them that makes them either negative or positive. The wise will not judge; they will just understand.

7

Is Hinduism feminist or patriarchal?

Like most religions, Hinduism is patriarchal. Unlike most religions, however, it is also feminist.

Generally, there are two types of feminism. Equality feminism believes that men and women are equal. Liberation feminism believes that women, like all humans, have a right to make decisions about their bodies, and their lives. Hinduism aligns more to 'liberation' feminism than to 'equality' feminism.

In fact, equality as an ideology has its roots in Christian mythology that rejected the notion of social hierarchy and considered all men (not women) equal in the eyes of God. This idea became popular roughly 1500 years ago when the Roman Empire turned Christian. In Islam equality is represented in the idea where all men who visit Mecca are expected to dress uniformly, despite belonging to diverse economic, political, national, racial and ethnic groups.

On another note: many Muslim women insist that the Quran gives women rights over property, though the social practice of Islam tends to be patriarchal. Likewise, Hinduism contains many feminist ideas that are frequently ignored, often deliberately, by patriarchs and also by atheist activists who *want* Hinduism to be patriarchal to justify their hatred of religion.

Many contemporary societies want to see people as humans, independent of all biology, including gender. 'Equality' feminists seek the same opportunities as men. This makes sense when the same labour is involved. Indra has to treat Durga as equal to Shiva or Vishnu if she kills an asura for him. But does that mean Durga is equal to Shiva, or Shiva is equal to Vishnu? Are they same, different, or unique?

Each deity has their unique personality and need. In 'equality' feminism, they are the same. But Shiva is content with raw milk, Vishnu needs processed milk and butter, while Durga demands blood. 'Liberation' feminism seeks that diversity to be acknowledged. In this feminism, Durga is not inferior to Shiva or Vishnu; nor superior, but they are different, each one unique, part of a diverse ecosystem.

In Hinduism, all creatures are equal in the sense that all of them are containers of atma. However, all creatures are diverse as the atma occupies different bodies. Atma is dehi, resident of the body, deha. Everyone's dehi is the same but our deha is different. Dehi is genderless but deha is gendered.

In art, the dehi is visualized as male and deha as female.

34   *Faith: 40 Insights into Hinduism*

This is metaphor. However, people take it literally and wrongly conclude that the spirit/mind/dehi is male and matter/body/deha is female.

Just as every plant is unique and nature has many categories of plants, every human is unique and culture has several categories of humans. Categories of the psychological (fourfold varna system of the Vedas), physiological (three-fold guna system of the Gita), social (thousand communities of the jati system). But the most important category is gender (male, female and others). Just as every plant has different food requirements, different humans need different things. Just as in a garden some plants are favoured over others, in society, some humans are given greater value than others. In some gardens, fruit-bearing trees are valued. In others flower-bearing trees are valued. Likewise, in some societies, the intellectual is valued, and in others the rich are valued. In some, men are valued, and in others, women are valued. Thus, different societies value different aspect of our body.

In Buddhism and Jainism, and Hindu monastic orders, the female body was considered inferior to the male body. To attain the highest knowledge, one had to take rebirth with a male body. This is because a male body creates life outside itself and a female body creates life inside itself. A male body can retain semen by mind control, however, a female body sheds menstrual blood which is outside mind control.

By contrast, in temple Hinduism, a god was seen as incomplete without a goddess. Shiva is incomplete without

Shakti, Krishna without Radha, Ram without Sita. The householder was a balancing force in society, not the single man or single woman. A single man could be respected only if he was celibate; the single woman if she attached herself to a deity, like Mirabai and Andal who loved Krishna, or Akkamahadevi who loved Shiva.

In early days, both celibate men and women were feared. Celibate men were feared as powerful and fierce yogis with magical powers who could only be controlled and made productive and calm through marriage. Likewise, unattached women were seen as sexual predators and fearful yoginis who could consume men, unless they were restrained by marriage and maternity. This may explain the cultural fear of independent women. The medieval Nath traditions, the celibate nath-jogi was in constant battle with the wild yoginis and matrikas, who could turn men into goats. Great value was accorded to the woman who chose to be faithful to one man (the sati), or who rejected her body altogether, like Karaikal Ammaiyar, the Tamil Saint, who became a shrivelled, gaunt, post-menopausal crone so she would not have to be a wife to her husband and could simply worship Shiva without being bothered by her body and its menstrual cycles. In later times, a celibate man became holy while unattached single women were seen as dangerous.

In Hinduism, all creatures exist within a framework of gender and caste, over which one has little or no control. We cannot choose what happens to us; that is determined by karma. But yoga is all about choosing how we react or respond to a situation. We have agency over our choices. We have to take responsibility for the consequences of our actions.

In the Manusmriti, we are told that a woman is subservient to men: to her father, brother, husband and son. She has to obey them. In other words, her agency is taken away from her. But in the Puranas, Sati and Parvati choose their own husbands and Lakshmi leaves Vishnu when she is not treated with respect. In the Mahabharata, Ganga and Satyavati lay down strict conditions before agreeing to marry. Usha even abducts her lover, Aniruddha, grandson of Krishna, in the Bhagavata. In the Ramayana, Sita insists she will follow her husband to the forest, despite his opposition. This suggests that the Manusmriti was never the 'supreme' code it is often made out to be. Women in Hindu narratives have displayed agency in various contexts, in keeping with 'liberation' feminism. However, unlike 'equality' feminism, you never see Parvati, Sati, Lakshmi, Ganga, Usha or Sita speaking of being oppressed by the men in their lives. There is no victim in Hindu mythology.

Yes, caste Hindus forbade widows from remarrying, but in the Ramayana the vanara-queen Tara remarries Sugriva and the rakshasa-queen Mandodari remarries Ravana, tales we don't highlight as these were practices of the 'lower' castes. The Vedas have no reference to sati and jauhar that have been glamorized by Bollywood and Rajput communities; but possibly these practices became popular only in medieval times. This was part of a global trend towards patriarchy. Yet, simultaneously, in many communities in India, there were women who were allowed to have multiple husbands and lovers, and even inheritance through women. But we do not talk about these as they are seen as 'inferior' castes. We must keep in mind that Hindu practices are not just practices of 'upper' castes. We must recognize the larger picture of myriad practices. In different communities, and at different times, women had different levels of agency.

The looking-at-the-world-through-the-lens-of-oppression idea has its roots in Greek mythology, where the hero is someone who challenges the whims of the gods, who control the fate of humans, and often a martyr who dies resisting. The glamorization of victimhood comes from Abrahamic mythology where the slaves of Egypt must be saved by the prophet from the evil Pharaoh, or one is continuously asked to mourn the death of Ali, son-in-law of the prophet. In Hinduism, by contrast, villains, whether it is Ravana (who does not care for Sita's consent) or Duryodhana (who publicly abuses Draupadi), are seen not as evil but as ignorant, insecure and faithless. A very different paradigm, one of constant tension, not vilification.

To deny any person agency, be it male or female, is to indulge our ego (aham). To value male flesh over female flesh is to value outer deha over the inner dehi. These are indicators of insecurity, and ignorance, that make us want to control and dominate. A wise man or woman will value dehi over deha, and always grant agency to all, not just men, so that the dehi can experience life to the fullest through the deha. Such a man or woman can be called a feminist. He, or she, is certainly not a patriarch.

Thus, we can safely say that Hinduism may seem patriarchal at a superficial level but has adequate fuel embedded in it to make it feminist.

8

Is a yogini a female yogi, or a wild, erotic witch?

The answer depends on what feelings are evoked in you by the words 'yogi', 'wild', 'erotic' and 'witch'. Are you revolted by words such as 'wild', 'erotic' and 'witch', or fascinated by them? Does 'yogi' induce a sense of equanimity resulting from letting go? Or does it conjure feelings of virtuous puritanism, associated with revulsion for sex and sensuality?

Some Hindus are (sadly) puritanical – ashamed of all things sexual. These are Victoria's children, still hung up in the nineteenth century, still striving hard to convince her that they are not effeminate, luxury-loving, sensuous Hindoos, but are mommy's good boys, who don't look at women *that* way. They are conditioned to be embarrassed of their desires and refuse to acknowledge women as autonomous sexual beings. A woman for them is only mother and sister. So, they deny the Tantrik aspect of Hinduism, where the divine feminine is central, and prefer to explain Hinduism through the filter of Middle American Christian or Middle Eastern Islamic fundamentalist groups where sex is sin (hence erotic is evil), and women are handmaidens of the devil (and must be tamed before they turn wild).

For the rest, who are comfortable with the divine feminine, a yogini opens the door to the Tantrik approach to wisdom, not via ritual as in the Mimansika, or the head as in Vedanta, or the heart as in Bhakti, but via the body, the rush of sensation, the pleasure, pain and the terror they evoke. If mantra, deals with the mind (mantra), then tantra deals with the body (tan). Due to its esoteric nature, Tantra has always shunned the mainstream, presenting its ideas in code instead (the first Tantrik texts emerge around 1400 years ago, though the tradition is much older), preferring oral transmission from teacher to student.

But first the word 'witch'.

The word 'witch' is a derogatory term used like the colloquial Hindi word 'dayan'. Both words refer to women (though there are male witches too) – a mage, a sorceress, who casts spells, and causes all kinds of problems like miscarriage, sickness in children, epidemics, infertility, wasting and impotency. People feared the knowledge these women possessed but also used it against their enemies. The word 'witch' may have its roots in pagan (pre-Christian) traditions, and probably referred to medicine women who knew how to use herbs and minerals to heal or harm. These women saw the forest as a Goddess and surrendered to her mysterious cycles. They refused to be part of mainstream society and preferred living alone, in communes, using men only as lovers, friends and assistants, rejecting the institution of marriage and the confinement that came with it. Mainstream society feared, but simultaneously respected and venerated these forest women.

The word 'dayan' probably comes from words like 'dakini' or 'dankuni' from folk Hindu and Tantrik Buddhist traditions, referring to wild goddesses associated with the forest, who are sexual and violent, a contrast to tamed, domestic, gentle goddesses. There was always tension between these women and mainstream society. With the rise of Christianity, these women were systematically massacred. Even today, in rural India, it is not uncommon to hear tales of women killed brutally after being accused of witchcraft. In Islamic communities, these women were associated with the dreaded djinns. In Victorian Europe, there were tales of the succubi who seduced men and stripped them of their virility. Similar tales of yakshinis are told in Kerala. Was the yakshini just another name for yogini? We can only wonder.

The yogini was very different from the yogi. While the yogi sought escape from both nature and culture, the yogini celebrated nature. This is evident in Buddhist, Hindu and Nath lore.

Buddhist lore speaks of goddesses such as Vajra-yogini, who is associated with Tantrik Buddhism and is visualized as a powerful goddess, wild and untamed, sexual and violent. She dances on top of corpses, holding a knife in one hand and a bowlful of blood in another and often sits on top of and copulates with the Bodhisattva – images that are known as Yab-Yum, or father-mother, in Tibetan Buddhism. Are these to be taken literally? Are these metaphors for the primordial union of female compassion and male wisdom? Are they images of secret Tantrik practices aimed to cause the reverse flow of semen in men via the spine? We can only speculate. But belief in these practices is strong in many Tantrik schools. If the images evoke Goddess Kali of Hinduism, it is not surprising, for Tantrik Buddhism and Hindu Shiva-Shakti traditions have a lot of in common.

Hindus built at least four temples to the collective of sixty-four yoginis, two in Odisha, at Hirapur and Ranipur-Jharial, and two in Madhya Pradesh, at Khajuraho and Bedaghat. These temples are unique in that they are circular and open air and the images of the sixty-four yoginis located in the periphery face inwards. In Hirapur, they are depicted standing on various vahanas. In Ranipur-Jharial, they dance. In Bedaghat, they sit. Their names reveal all kinds of women: from the female form of male gods (Aindri, Varahi, Vaishnavi) to independent goddesses (Kali, Chinnamastika), from benevolent goddesses (Lakshmi) to malevolent goddesses (Birupa); some young, some old, some desirable, others hideous. The whole spectrum of femininity is thus celebrated, not just what is deemed appropriate for culture. This tradition has been completely overshadowed today by the celebration of celibate male ascetics who reject all things feminine.

In Nath lore, yoginis are powerful women with magical powers, usually belonging to so-called 'lower' castes, who work as washerwomen, potters, weavers and crematorium attendants. They are in conflict with the celibate monks with yogic powers that are attained through celibacy (siddha). So, there are tales of how Gorakhnath rescued his guru, Matsyendranath, for the realm of women who enchanted him to give up the life of a hermit. And there are tales of the war between Jalendranath and the yoginis who turn Jalendranath's disciples into donkeys, much like Circe of Greek mythology. Are these real stories? Fantasies of a culture uncomfortable with women who refuse to bow to men? Or sacred stories revealing the tension between male celibacy and female sexuality? We can only speculate.

Some Hindus refute the existence of these stories. They even claim they are not part of 'pure' Hinduism. They feel especially angry when female academicians (perhaps in mischief, or in the spirit of genuine research) point to these stories and pull them down from their high puritanical horses. It's the same male indignation that we see on the Internet against strong, aggressive, assertive feminists. The presence of yoginis informs us that Hinduism is vast and varied, and not just the stronghold of male, puritanical Brahmins and hermits.

9

What are Hindu views on death, and suicide?

The world across, what happens after death can be divided into two schools of thought. Those who believe in one life and those who believe in multiple lives. Hinduism belongs to the latter.

Those who believe you live only once can be further categorized into those who believe death is the end, there is nothing else after that; those who believe that after death you go to the land of the dead and stay in the afterlife forever; and those who believe that after death you go either to heaven, where you enjoy the rest of eternity, or to hell, where you suffer for all eternity (or maybe until you have been adequately punished and are ready to join others in heaven).

Rationalists believe death is the end and so are in a hurry to solve all problems of life in this – their one and only – life.

Ancient Egyptians built pyramids because they believed in an eternal afterlife. Ancient Chinese, before Buddhism introduced the idea of rebirth, believed in the land of ancestors where one went after death. Even today, there are rituals in which paper money is offered to ancestors to spend in the land of the dead, from whence there is no return. Christians and Muslims believe in heaven and hell; where one ends up depends on whether one has lived one's only life as per the code of God.

Those who believe in rebirth believe you keep coming back from the land of the dead (pitr-loka) to the land of the living (bhu-loka) until you learn the ultimate lesson after which you no longer feel the need for a body. There are variations on this, where you are punished for various crimes in hell (naraka-loka) before you are ready to be reborn, or where you enjoy heaven (swarga-loka) until it is time for you to return to earth once again.

While re-birth (punar-janam) and re-death (punar-mrityu) are seen as inevitable, Hindus also believe in the concept of immortality (amrita). The devas who live in the sky and the asuras who live under the earth fight over this nectar, as do birds (garuda) and snakes (naga). The asuras have sanjivani vidya, by which they can resurrect the dead. This is used by Jayanta to bring Shukra back to life. In the Mahabharata, serpents have the naga-mani, or serpent jewel, that can bring back the dead to life; this is used to bring Arjuna back to life after he is slain by Babruvahana.

Historically, in the Vedas, we do not find a clear reference to rebirth. There is reference to how our body, after it dies, returns to nature, just like the primordial purusha – his eye becomes the sun, his breath becomes the wind. There is reference to something that outlives death: atman, jiva, manas, prana. There is reference to a happy land of ancestors and gods (swarga) and to the land of pain (naraka) below the three heavens. There is reference to feeding the ancestors (pitr). But the idea of rebirth as we know it today is not formed in the Vedas.

The idea of rebirth evolves in the Upanishads and is fully expressed in the Puranas. While the Vedic householders believed that performing yagnas and one's worldly duties (dharma) took one to heaven, the Vedic hermits spoke of the karma theory, of immortality, of uniting the individual self (atma, jiva-atma) with the cosmic self (brahman, param-atma) through meditation (dhyana), austerities (tapasya) and various social, mental and physical exercises (yoga).

What we find are two options merging: return to this world in another form, or escape to another world. Hence, Hindu rituals are a combination of fire (for escape) and water (for rebirth). Some communities even choose burial. There are communities that feed ancestors in rituals (shradh) and promise to help their rebirth. In this ritual, we focus on the relationship of food (anna) and flesh (anna-kosha), and how the dead yearn to return to the land of the living, have a body and consume food, while striving for liberation.

Then there is the concept of voluntary renunciation of the body (samadhi), which rationalists argue is actually self-termination of life after fulfilling one's worldly duties.

For example, Ram in the Ramayana walks into the river Sarayu and does not rise again after he passes his kingdom on to his children. Likewise, the Pandavas walk away into mountains after passing their kingdom on to the next generation. Some argue this is ritual voluntary suicide after discharging one's worldly duties.

Since suicide is a sin in Christianity, in keeping with its colonial legacy, attempting suicide, in India, was illegal and punishable – until recently, when the law was made more sympathetic. Indians have always had a mature relationship with death. It is perfectly fine to willingly give up one's life, after completing all worldly duties, with the permission of one's family. Though controversial today, it is a common theme in the Puranas. Hence the concept of sanyasa-ashrama, the final stage of life, when you renounce the world and its bindings and focus on the divine.

10

Does Hinduism have anything to say about cognition?

irst, what is cognition? It is the process by which we make sense of the world: the act of sensing, observing, that leads to the emergence of various feelings and thoughts in our selves about the external world. Different words are used for cognition in Hindu, Buddhist and Jain scriptures, such as 'chitta', 'prana', 'jiva', and 'atma', often interchangeably. There is an obsession with these words in Indian thought. And it is a distinguishing feature of Indian philosophy. At the heart of this are the observer and the observed, that which sees, and that which is seen, perceiver and perceived, seer and seen, mind and matter, dehi and deha.

Cognitive science is rapidly emerging as a field of study in modern science in universities around the world. However, this was not always the case. The mind was not as important as matter in the early days of science. In fact, nineteenth century society was built on ideas such as objectivity, hence engineering, where hardly any value is placed on perception. In fact, perception was a bad word. Science viewed emotions and subjectivity as inferior. However, in recent times, more people have begun to value the role of perceptions, emotions and subjectivity in the creative and cultural process. Therefore, the engineering mindset is slowly being replaced by the design mindset, which considers creative subjectivity. Hence, value is being placed increasingly on cognitive sciences, the systematic study of how we become aware of the world around us. This has led many scientists to appreciate ancient Indian thought.

Hinduism, Buddhism and Jainism give as much value to cognition, as Judaism, Christianity and Islam give to the commandments. This can be seen as the fundamental difference between the two. The former speaks about how we perceive the world, and how we can change our perception of the world; the latter speaks of how we are supposed to behave in the world. The word 'spirituality', which is about self-discovery, leans towards the former and the word 'religion', which is about social engineering, leans towards the latter.

European, American, and Left-wing academicians, have tried very hard to contort Hinduism as a 'commandment' religion – with commandments coming from the Vedas, Gita, Manusmriti, which in turn creates the caste system. Therefore, they believe new commandments, like the reservation policy, will annihilate the caste system, when, in fact, it does the very opposite, by further entrenching it.

Right wing radicals (they are mostly 'upper' caste men) who oppose them, rather ironically, simply seek a new set of commandments that allows them to stay in a dominant position. In doing so, they are structurally aligned to the Western reading of Hinduism, more about commandments than cognition.

Ancient Indians differentiated between nature (prakriti) and culture (sanskriti). Both prakriti and sanskriti are realms of shape (akar) and shape (akruti) around us. However, prakriti is the default design, while sanskriti is design indicative of human intervention, the presence of dehi. The extent of cultural refinement is an indicator of the extent of human awareness. Refinement was achieved through rites of passage (sanskar) such as upbringing, education, marriage, social obligations and funeral rites, that distinguish us from animals. 'Sanskar', the word, reveals the human desire to give design (akar) to the default natural world of life and death (sansara, or sansar).

The Rig Veda introduces us to our mind (brah-mana); Sama Veda to the domesticating process as it distinguishes between forest (aranya) and settlement (grama); and Yajur Veda to the relationship as it focuses on yagna, the ritual 'exchange' where something is given (svaha) to the gods in the hope that they will give us what we desire (tathastu). Europeans perceived this exchange as a sacrifice, resulting in a total misunderstanding of this fundamental human ritual for the past 200 years. Any economist will tell you that exchange creates a fair society based on reciprocity; sacrifice simply leads to exploitation.

The Atharva Veda spoke of everyday life with codes of conduct and spells to attract fortune and be rid of misfortune. The fifth veda was the Natya-shastra which spoke of stories, songs, art and performances, of aesthetic experiences (rasa) and emotional churning (bhava) that make us truly cultured.

Refined language (Sanskrit) was supposed to be an indicator a human (manava) with an expanded mind (brah-mana) as opposed someone who was still elemental and spoke organic languages (Prakrit) of the marketplace. This is why Ram is impressed to see Hanuman, a creature of the forest, speaking chaste Sanskrit. Yet, the reverse is not true. The Ramayana warns us that language alone is not indicative of refinement; for Ravana speaks chaste Sanskrit and is a scholar of the Vedas (veda-acharya), yet behaves like a brute when he abducts another man's wife and gives greater value to his desires over a woman's will.

The word for refinement, sanskriti, (often pronounced samskriti) is a combination of two words: 'sama' and 'akriti'. Sama draws attention to the musical sama, the end and beginning of a musical cycle, the return to the first note, indicating how refinement has a lot to do with cyclical thinking, coming back to the origin. We see this sound in words like equanimity (sama-chitta), dialogue (sama-vada), unravelling (sama-adhi). For refinement involves uncrumpling the mind from a state of nervousness that makes us self-serving (aham) and bringing it to the state of confidence that makes us unconditionally generous (atma). In the state of aham, we are like animals, seeking domination, and being territorial. In the state of atma, we seek to rise above animal instincts: we give, rather than grab; we receive rather than take; we appreciate the finiteness of existence yet the infinity of the world.

Purity (shuddhi) is not removing impurities in the outside world of matter; it is removing impurities in the world of the mind. Impure crumpled minds seek purity outside, hence practice untouchability and consider menstruation as dirty. Purified uncrumpled expanded refined minds see purity everywhere, and do not view Brahmin as superior to Shudra, or men as superior to women, or heterosexuals as superior to homosexuals, or cis-gendered people as superior to trans-gendered people. He who moves out of limited reality (mithya) towards limitless reality (satya) is free even when alive (jiva-mukta).

In early Vedic scriptures, consciousness (atma), emotions (chitta), indriya (senses) and life (jiva) are used interchangeably. Even today, exact meanings remain elusive. But all forms of enquiry (mimansa) began by understanding life and the living body, what distinguishes the inorganic (ajiva, achit) from organic (jiva, chit), the elemental (bhuta) from life-forms that are mobile, i.e. animals (chara) and life-forms that immobile, i.e. plants (achara). In a Vedic pancha-yagna, we are asked to be cognizant of all forms of existence: the elemental, the living (fixed, moving, realized) and even the dead. We are asked to be aware of the self (jiva-atma), the other (para-atma) and the cosmic (param-atma).

Hunger distinguishes the living from the non-living. Jiva seeks food and so needs sense organs (gyan indriya) and action organs (karma indriya). Fear is obvious in animals more than plants as prey avoid being consumed by predators. Neither the fixed tree (achara) nor the moving animal (chara) wants to be consumed (bali). Yet both yearn for food (bhoga). Thus, life feeds on life (jivo jivatsya jivanam) as stated in the Bhagavata Purana. This creates the law of the jungle (matsya nyaya) – where the mighty feed on the meek. Hunger and fear distinguish the organic from the inorganic. Hunger and fear are what create the animal and plant kingdoms of nature. They create the herd, the hive and the pack, the food chain and the pecking order. The observer (rishi) thus appreciates the diversity of nature and the cognitive principles underlying it. This nature when domesticated and controlled and improved upon creates culture.

Culture is all about domesticating fire (yagna-sthala), domesticating water using ponds (kunda) and pots (kumbha), domesticating plants (kshetra), animals (vahana) and humans (dharma) such that they reject the law of the jungle, and use their strength to protect the weak, and their wealth to feed the hungry. Only when we have excess resources, when we are well fed and secure, do we seek to nourish our other senses with song and dance and entertainment. And through them seek the meaning of the deeper issues of life.

All conversations of rasa, and bhava, and indriya where sensations are registered, and chitta where emotions are churned, take us to the body. And traditionally, Indians visualized the body as a series of layers or sheaths or circles (kosha) such as anna-kosha (circle of flesh), prana-kosha (circle of breath), indriya-kosha (circle of senses), chitta-kosha (circle of emotions), buddhi-kosha (circle of intelligence). The body being seen as a series of concentric realms maps itself to the various activities of yoga that seek to uncrumple the mind (chitta-vritti-nirodha).

Here the body is seen as having a physical layer (sthula sharira) and a psychological layer (sukshma sharira) and an external 'karmic' layer of the world around us (karana sharira), full of objects and relationships, some that we call our own (mine) and some that we do not call our own (not mine; yours, his, hers, theirs). Deep within, and far beyond, is the atma, the formless (nirakara) and attribute-less (nirguna) conceptual reality that we refer to in English as the spirit and the soul, and which perhaps under the increasingly Islamic and Christian influence of the last 1000 years, we identified as God.

The eight-fold path of yoga was a systematic journey from outside to inside, from the social body through the physical body into the psychological body as revealed by the steps of yoga, such as yama (relationship discipline), niyama (self-discipline), asana (posture discipline), pranayama (breath training), pratyahara (sense discipline), dharana (mind expansion to develop perspective), dhyana (mind contraction to develop focus) and finally samadhi (mind discipline to let go of things, having realized the self does not does seek property). Thus everything is connected.

But what distinguishes humans from the rest of nature? This question is key to Indian thought. The oldest Indian philosophy is known as enumeration (sankhya, or samkhya). It lists the basic categories of the world. It distinguishes humanity (purusha) from nature (prakriti). Under prakriti, it lists the non-cognitive (bhuta) and all aspects of cognition (indriya, chitta, buddhi, manas). What is purusha then? It is identified with the formless (nirakara) and attribute-less (nirguna): atma, brahman. Buddha rejected this category. He focussed on emptiness (shunya). Shankar saw atma is everything, completeness (purna) or infinity (ananta). This remains the fundamental difference between Buddhism and Hinduism.

But Vedanta's quest for the essence of humanity through negation (neti-neti, not this, not that) is complemented by Tantra's quest through affirmation (iti-iti, this too, that too). Tantra notices that there is a pattern within diversity. From creatures (microbes) with senses but without emotions to creatures (lower animals) with senses and emotions but not intelligence, to creatures (higher animals) with senses and emotions and intelligence but not imagination, and finally creatures (humans) with senses, emotions, intelligence and imagination. It acknowledges that in humans, you have something that no other animal has – the ability to conceptualize abstract thoughts, analyse, hypothesize and create knowledge that is transmitted over generations. Thus, over generations, a family of chimpanzees does not change much, but a family of humans does change, because of the transmission of conceptualized knowledge. And all this happens because of imagination. Human birth (manushya-yoni) is special.

It is significant that imagination is not given much value in either philosophical as well as scientific conversations.

Until recent times, imagination was a bad word. But rooted in imagination is humanity. In fact, in ancient Tantra, we realize siddha (magical powers) is about seeking things that we can only imagine – the ability to fly, walk on water, change size and shape and weight at will, and attract, manipulate and dominate everything around us.

Classically, in tribal society, knowledge systems tend to tilt towards stagnation. In non-tribal societies, there is a shift towards development. In the Bhagavata Purana, the wild self-absorbed King Vena's body is churned. Two beings emerge: the tribal (nishadha) who goes to the forest and the dharma-establishing king (Prithu) who governs a society based on varna-ashrama-dharma, the four-fold division of society (acknowledgement of political and economic hierarchy in social groups) and phase of life (acknowledgement of social dynamism through old age and death). This is different form modern society where development means improving material reality rather than psychological reality.

Today development is all about things rather than thoughts, about creating effectiveness and efficiency in the world around us, rather than about becoming caring and compassionate. Science is geared to removing hunger and fear by creating more food and weapons, but it has not been able to eliminate either hunger or war, as it does not consider the mind important. This is where 'dharma' played a key role.

In conclusion, it is important to return to the earlier point of difference between cognition and commandment. The West saw, and continues to see, caste in terms of commandment.

But the scriptures saw caste in terms of cognition. While the Westernized mind believes policy changes will annihilate caste, Indian wisdom believes only the expansion of one's mind/cognition/awareness/consciousness will end the need for hierarchies.

Faith: 40 Insights into Hinduism

11

Is karma fatalism?

The word 'karma' occurs in the Rig Samhita, the earliest collection of Vedic verses. But there it means activity, specifically ritual activity. It is not related to the result of the action. In other words, karma means action, but not reaction. It means sowing the seed, in the Vedas. In the Upanishads, it also means the production of a subsequent fruit. This later meaning is perhaps embedded in the early use of the word also because the karma that is being spoken of is the ritual act of conducting yagna. Yagna involves svaha (input) that results in tathastu (output).

The West equates karma with destiny and accuses Indians of being fatalistic and complacent because of their faith in karma. Such views are based not on the wrong understanding but on the incomplete understanding of karma. A deeper understanding of karma will reveal that it is also the force that makes us extremely proactive and responsible. The West's understanding of karma is based on the biblical expression: 'as you sow, so you reap', which is deterministic and based on certainty. But in Hinduism. karma is based on the Gita's wisdom: 'focus on actions, not results', which is non-deterministic and based on uncertainty.

This shift in the meaning of karma, from mere action, to action that causes reaction, is attributed to shramanas (hermit thinkers) who refused to be mere samsaris (householder ritualists). They lived around 500 BCE, known as the Axis Age, the age that also saw the rise of Socratic thought in Greece, Confucian thought in China and Zoroastrian thought in Persia. The thinkers of India included Yagnavalkya, who was married to two women, as well as Sakyamuni Buddha and Vardhamana Mahavira, both of whom gave up marriage and family to become monks. Yagnavalkya, despite his radical thoughts, did not break free from the brahmanical ritual fold and was hence deemed astika, one who believes in the value of the yagna. Buddha started the Buddhist monastic order while Mahavira was seen as a leader of the much older austere Jain order. Both of them were called nastikas, those who do not believe in the value of the yagna.

Vaishyas (traders) felt slighted by Brahmins who preferred to see Kshatriyas (kings) as their primary patrons. So many in the mercantile community turned to shramanas who seemed more egalitarian. They perhaps contributed to the understanding of karma, for much of karma theory resonates trading practices such as being in debt and receiving returns on investment.

Every action came to be seen eventually as an investment, and its outcome the return on investment. Good investments meant good returns, bad investments meant bad returns.

But who knows what action is good and what action is bad? Yes, karma may be about reaping the fruit of the seed we sow but you may think you are sowing the seed of a sweet mango but it is quite possible that the fruit will turn out to be a sour tamarind or a fiery chilli. A king was once given a fruit which, if consumed by his wife, would enable her to bear him a child. The king had two wives and so he gave each one half the fruit. As a result, both queens gave birth to half a child. Thus, the action (dividing the fruit to be fair to both wives) was good but the reaction (half a child per wife) was bad. Likewise, a thief who climbed to the high branches of a tree to avoid capture was blessed by a deity because flowers from the tree accidentally fell on the image of the deity under the tree. This made karma unpredictable, much like market investments.

People have long tried to classify actions as good karma and bad karma, but the fact is bad actions (paap) are usually called so in hindsight when the outcome is negative. Likewise, good actions (punya) become so in hindsight when the outcome is positive. At the point of action, we do not know whether the results will favour us or not. Thus, we can control only our actions, not the reactions, or how the future will judge our actions. This point is amplified by Krishna in the Bhagavad Gita in response to Arjuna's query on karma.

Karma presupposes rebirth. Our current situation in life is a reaction to actions in our past life. That is why some people are born poor, ugly and to horrible parents. The West points to this belief as the cause of India's complacency, that by attributing current circumstances to fate, rather than to social injustice, we are removing the motivation to strive or fight. What is overlooked is that the word 'fate' comes from the Fates, three Greek goddesses who spun the yarn of mortal life and who, on the advice of Zeus, king of Olympian gods, determined how long the thread should be, and when it should be cut.

Those who genuinely believe in karma know that just as the past determines the present, the present determines the future. Thus, to secure the future, one works hard in the present. In other words, genuine belief in karma should make a person more proactive and responsible. If a person chooses to be lazy instead, it has nothing to do with karma but it has everything to do with laziness.

In fact, the idea of karma yoga rose in response to monastic practices that were seen as promoting inaction. Philosophies were elaborated to cope with the fear of karmic consequence and continue to perform duties as householders. These philosophies declared that inaction was also an action, an act of omission that would have consequences. He who fought could kill the killer. He who did not fight enabled the killer to strike another victim. Thus, no monk could escape from karma. To liberate oneself from the web of karma, one had to develop the mental equilibrium to worldly circumstances, aware but unperturbed by good or bad circumstances and outcomes.

Thus, karma determines the current circumstances of our life. How we choose to react to past karma is our choice. We may choose to accept it or change it. Our choices may be deemed good by some and bad by others, right by some, wrong by others, but these ethical and moral qualifications have no impact on the consequences of our action, and the impact on our future circumstances. Whatever has to happen, will happen, our desires notwithstanding.

The West rejects the idea of rebirth. Both the religious and the rational West believes that a child is born with a clean karmic balance sheet. That when a person dies the balance sheet is settled. There is no carry forward. Not so in Hinduism, Buddhism and Jainism, where there is an unsettled account at the time of birth and an unsettled account at the time of death. The former comes from the previous life and the latter leads to the next life.

The West with its fixation on clarity, conviction and confidence finds such Indian explanations of the karma concept exasperating. Thus, it rejects all Indian definitions, and prefers one-dimensional Western ones that reduce karma to fatalism. In Hinduism, however, karma is both fatalism (accepting circumstances) and responsibility (choosing a response to a circumstance based either on insecurity or wisdom).

12

Is Buddha an avatar of Vishnu?

Buddhism rose in India 2500 years ago. It played a key role in spreading monastic ideas across the country. Before Buddhism, the focus on religious life was in the form of the yagna ritual in which the gods were invoked for material gains. Great value was placed on social obligations such as marriage, and children. Meditative ideas were restricted to the scholarly communities. Buddha changed the rules of the game and discussed ideas of desire and suffering with the common man, inviting them to join the community (sangha) of monks and live in monasteries (viharas) where one could acquire wisdom (bodhi) that would grant peace and freedom. This became highly popular. The old ways were being abandoned.

Thus Vedic Hinduism reframed itself to become Puranic Hinduism. While Buddhist scholars focussed on negation of life, zero (shunya), Hindu storytellers spoke of affirmation of life, infinity (ananta). Life was full of joy and pleasure. The wise was not one who renounced the world; the wise was one who participated in the world, without getting attached to it. Stories of such wise men were retold in epics such as the Ramayana and the Mahabharata. In temples, rituals celebrated the marriage of gods and goddesses. Beauty and pleasure were displayed on temple walls. People spoke of the wise god, Vishnu, who preserves the social order, and does not destroy it as monks do.

Although Brahma creates the social order, he and his children (Indra, for example) are not at peace with the world. Shiva renounces the social order, becomes a hermit, and is at peace. Shakti marries Shiva and gets him to participate in social life, but he remains a reluctant householder, unable to appreciate social norms. Vishnu is a fruitful member of society, taking various mortal forms (avatar), sometimes priest (Vamana), sometimes king (Ram), sometimes cowherd (Krishna), living life fully, wisely, as he is enlightened in the ways of the Veda.

Clearly, for over a 1000 years, Buddhism and Hinduism were rivals. But they influenced each other's philosophies and mythologies. For instance, Adi Shankaracharya was accused of being Prachanna Bauddha, masking Buddhist ideas in Vedic lore, and the Buddhist concept of heaven and hell reveal a strong Puranic influence.

Initially, followers of the Vedas (Nigama traditions) were opposed to followers of the Puranas (Agama traditions) as they valued the yagna rituals over the puja rituals of the temple.

But gradually, the Nigama and Agama schools merged, and the brahmachari-sanyasi-acharyas became heads of monastic orders as well as temples. This happened from about 1000 years ago. Around this time, Buddha started being seen as an avatar of Vishnu. However, this Buddha was not Gautama Buddha of the Buddhists.

The value placed on householders by Hindus, led to the transformation of old Theravada Buddhism into Mahayana Buddhism where greater value was placed on the Bodhisattva, who is more compassionate and understanding of human material desires than the enlightened Buddha. The value given to hermits by Buddhists led to the transformation of householder-based Vedic Hinduism into hermit-based Puranic Hinduism. Gurus who embraced celibacy and renunciation such as Shankara and Ramanuja created monastic orders (mathas) much like Buddhist viharas. Buddhists told stories of how the Adi Buddha manifests himself as Buddhas and Bodhisattvas for the benefit of humanity, an idea mirrored by the increasingly popular concept of avatar found among Puranic Hindus. The presence of Goddess Tara in later Buddhism was clearly a Tantrik influence. Thus, for a long time, Hinduism and Buddhism mingled and merged.

It must be kept in mind that this differentiation between Hinduism and Buddhism did not matter to the common man who worshipped both simultaneously and did not distinguish much between the two. In Thailand, we find temples that celebrate Buddha and Ram simultaneously as aspects of the same discourse. The divide mattered to the Brahmin community, and to the monastic orders, who were rivals seeking royal patronage for their rituals and temples, and for the monasteries. Also, words like Hinduism and Buddhism that we use today emerged in colonial times, in the nineteenth century. Before that the words used were more caste based. The argument was whether one followed the ways of Buddha or those of Brahma (i.e. the Vedas) or Shiva and Vishnu (i.e. the Puranas).

In some texts, such as the Bhagavata Purana, Vishnu takes the form of a hermit to trick asuras away from Vedic rituals, enabling the devas to defeat them. Here, the hermit is associated with Buddha as well as Jina (from the monastic Jainism, another rival religion). In other texts, such as the Gita Govinda, Vishnu takes the form of a hermit to save animals from animal sacrifices, drawing attention to the idea that at least some Vedic sacrifices involved offering of animals (an idea that many orthodox Hindus reject and consider a wrong interpretation). In time, Vishnu's ninth avatar, the hermit, came to be seen by some as Buddha and by some as Jina. This was perhaps a strategic move to get more Buddhists and Jains to embrace Vaishnavism, and later Hinduism.

For Buddhists, Sakyamuni Buddha was a historical figure who lived 2500 years ago, and a metaphysical figure (Adi Buddha) who manifests as the compassionate Bodhisattva for the benefit of humanity. There is no Vishnu, or Shiva, in their worldview. Different truths exist in different periods of history and different geographies of the world. We need to respect the faith of the faithful, rather than impose our views on them as to who Buddha really was or was not. And it is also important to recognize the politics underlying such assertions.

One can therefore say, for Buddhists, Buddha is not an avatar of Vishnu; but, for Hindus, he probably is.

13

Is Hinduism's Narasimha like Hollywood's Wolverine?

An avatar is not a superhero. A superhero is not an avatar.

Narasimha is an avatar of Vishnu. The Puranas describe him as being half-human and half-lion. Wolverine is a tortured superhero. The Marvel universe describes him as a mutant. The two are very different from each other.

An avatar is God who takes mortal form to help humanity. Narasimha is the form taken by Vishnu to kill an asura (often translated as demon in English) who cannot be killed by a human or an animal, which means he can only be killed by someone who is neither fully human nor fully animal – like Narasimha. Unlike a superhero, an avatar does not go on any adventures. An avatar has full knowledge of the future and of the opponent, and is playing a role, hence the word 'leela' or the play of God.

A superhero, by contrast, is a mortal human who acquires superhuman powers, thus becoming extraordinary. And he or she uses these special powers to help humanity. The superhero is based on the mythological Greek hero like Heracles – different from other mortals as one of his parents is a god from Olympus – who goes on adventures, realizes his destiny and, on the way, helps humanity. Wolverine is one such superhero, a mutant, with keen-animal senses, great strength, three retractable claws in each hand, and of course super-regenerative powers that make him a near immortal and invincible. An angry frustrated loner, a failed samurai archetype, he struggles with his dark side as he tries to do good, and be good, albeit not always successfully.

In modern video games, the word 'avatar' is used as a duplicate identity, a mask to hide who you really are. This is how the West makes sense of a Hindu mythic concept. It is common for many Western writers to force-fit ideas from other cultures into a Western template. And so, for them, an avatar is the Hindu version of a superhero.

Who is the beneficiary of this play-acting? The so-called villain. For instance, in the story of Narasimha, the asura who is slain is not being punished; he is being liberated from a curse. The asura, Hiranakashipu, was the doorkeeper of Vishnu's abode in his previous life and was cursed to become an asura for a lifetime because he stopped a sage from entering while Vishnu was slept. Vishnu, by killing Hiranakashipu, is liberating him from the asura form. Thus, the story of an avatar demands belief in karma, and rebirth. The story of a

Greek hero, or superhero, demands no such belief. In fact, the assumption is that the superhero has only one life to prove his worth as a problem-solver and to redeem himself, as in the case of Wolverine, who must rid himself of his nasty past

Thus, a superhero is an ordinary man who becomes extraordinary. His journey is from small to big. By contrast, an avatar is the limitless divine (Vishnu) who becomes the limited divine (Narasimha, or any other avatar). His journey is from big to small. Both benefit humanity. In the superhero's case, it's a choice: the alternative is to be a super-villain. In the avatar's case, benefitting humanity is the whole point.

We often seek similarities between Indian and Western stories. But we must probe the reason. Is it to prove that Indians measure up to Western standards? A desire most often seen in people with an inferiority complex about India. Or is it to say that the modern West is imitating the path charted by India's past? A common idea in people with a superiority complex about all things Indian. Or is it to show that Indians and Westerners are no different? As people who refuse to recognize the cultural difference want.

Different beliefs surrounding cultures create the differences between them. Indian culture revolves around the belief in rebirth; this makes it comfortable with diversity, and uncertainty and subjectivity. The world here is fluid and the avatar is patient with human insecurity born of incomplete knowledge. Western culture revolves around the belief in one life, which makes it comfortable with equality, certainty and objectivity. Their world here is fixed and can only change if there is a revolution, which the superhero brings about. A superhero is needed in a world filled with problems. An avatar is needed in a world without wisdom.

Faith: 40 Insights into Hinduism

14

Why are Brahmin and Kshatriya, even Vaishya, aspirational for most, but not Shudra?

The chatur-varna system or the four-fold division of society was a key feature of Vedic society. The four tiers were the sources of Vedic lore (the Brahmins), the controllers of land (the Kshatriyas), the regulators of the markets (the Vaishyas) and the providers of various services (the Shudras). This was not a true reflection of society, but a speculation of what constitutes any society.

In practice, Indian society has long been divided into jatis. There are thousands of jatis, as against four varnas. When people say caste, they are referring to a European term used to explain jati, not varna. We often confuse the two. Jati was an economic-political unit, based on vocation. You inherited your jati from your father. Jati was established by a relatively simple idea called 'roti-beti': you ate with members of your

or clan

own jati, and you married a boy or girl from your own jati. A jati functioned like a tribe. Just as inter-tribe marriages are not permitted, inter-jati marriages were also not permitted. Crossing jati lines could lead to violence.

Genetic studies have revealed that the jati system became rigid 1900 years ago while the Vedas are over 3000 years old. Which suggests that the Vedas do refer to social diversity as a principle but do not speak of inflexible hierarchical communities.

The relative position of a person in society in a hierarchy, was determined by regional realities. For example, the jati of Kayasthas in the Gangetic plains emerged with the rise of Hindu bureaucrats in Mughal courts. Not many people in south India would know how to locate a Kayastha in their community. Likewise, few in Rajasthan would understand who the Lingayats of Karnataka were, and where they stood in the caste hierarchy, considering they reject the caste system.

Many people say that India's caste system is simply a rational division of labour to promote efficiency and effectiveness. Those who say this usually associate themselves with the top two tiers (Brahmin and Kshatriya), less commonly with the third tier (Vaishya) and hardly ever with the fourth tier (Shudra). However, if anyone says 'I am proud to be a Shudra', it is more from a sense of rebellion than wisdom or affection. And if people are proud to be Brahmin and Kshatriya, it has more to do with the desire to be dominant and less to do with wisdom or affection.

As a rule of thumb, those involved in priestly matters were Brahmins, and those who controlled the land were Kshatriyas.

But where did the bureaucrat who served in the king's court fit in? Was he Brahmin or Kshatriya or simply a Shudra, a service-provider? New warlords who came from outside like the Sakas and Pallavas and settled in India were anointed as Kshatriyas and linked to the gods and to Puranic kings to grant them legitimacy. A rich moneylender was a Vaishya but was he not a service-provider as well, providing banking services? And was a mercenary, who owned no land, and sold his military services to the highest bidder, a Kshatriya or a Shudra? Mapping the thousands of jatis to the four varnas has always been a challenge. In the south, Brahmins became powerful by controlling many farmlands – the Brahmadeya villages and Agraharas. But did that not make them landowners and hence Kshatriyas? Were the Peshwas of Maharashtra Brahmins or Kshatriyas or administration service-providers? These were complex matters that inevitably led to quarrels.

The Vedas do speak of a diverse society. The dominant members of society, the Brahmins, the landowners, the rich and the powerful, turned this concept of diversity into a hierarchical society. They did it using the dharma-shastras. In the dharma-shastras, including the Manusmriti, the Brahmin jatis mapped themselves to the Brahmin varna. They were not interested in mapping the thousands of other jatis.

There was a hierarchy among the Brahmin jatis too. The one who chanted Vedic lore saw themselves as superior to those who worked as purohits in temples. Those who performed marriages were seen as superior to those who performed funerals. Likewise, there was a hierarchy among Kshatriyas,

Vaishyas and Shudras. This hierarchy came not from any scripture but from regional politics.

Every society in the world has economic and political hierarchies. What makes the jati system unique is the hierarchy of purity. Some service-providers were deemed 'dirty' and denied access to the village well and even human dignity. This is the worst aspect of the caste system, something that is often denied by apologists. Was this recommended by the Vedas? No, it was not. The Vedas spoke of atma, the soul, that is eternally pure, and values diversity, not hierarchy. They spoke of fear and ignorance that nourishes the aham, the ego, which values flesh and various hierarchies.

The Muslim kings of India did not bother with the jati system as long as they were treated as Kshatriyas. The other, non-royal Muslims gained status in their villages depending on the vocation they followed and how much wealth they had.

It was the British who, as part of the first census, tried to formally map the various jatis to the four varnas and it was a messy process as they realized that many communities of India did not have clear cut jatis. A farmer in summer would be a soldier in winter – was he Kshatriya or Vaishya (if he owned the land) or Shudra (if was landless)? The documentation of caste by the British fixed a relatively fluid system, and sought to establish an awkward singular national hierarchy which was distinct from the multiple regional hierarchies. This documentation played a key role in drawing attention to the plight of the Dalit community. But it also demanded the construction of artificial hierarchies where once none had existed. In newly emerging urban ecosystems, where it would have been easy to wipe out old caste identities, caste documents ensured the persistence of village prejudices.

After Independence, the reservation policy ensured the continuance of the hierarchy between jatis as it assumed that some jatis did not deserve positive discrimination and some did. And so poor members of the so-called 'upper' castes suffered due to the excesses of rich members of their own castes. Likewise, no one realized that many members of the so-called 'lower' castes were richer and more privileged as they lived in urban areas. Attempts to homogenize Hinduism have failed as the reality of the diversity of jatis persists and the assumed role of varnas demands satisfaction.

Today the jati hierarchy is being reinforced by political ideologies that want to split the thousands of jatis of India into two boxes: the oppressors and the oppressed, the privileged and the unprivileged, savarna and Dalit. The doctrine of social justice is so combative that it ends up reinforcing hierarchies. Activists and politicians will not let you escape the Dalit or the savarna tag, whether you want to or not, for as a member of a jati you are part of a vote bank as well as part of a mob.

We do not mind being a servant (dasa) of God or guru, but not of other people because of the feudal mindset. And we fear equality because it strips us of identity and status, and dissolves us into a homogenous social personality. Like the Brahmins of yore, and the British, and the government, we continue to map ourselves on the theoretical, basic four-layered society of the Vedas, often to feel good about ourselves.

Until the Industrial Revolution, every society was controlled by the intellectual elite (priests and philosophers), the landed gentry and the mercantile class. The rest were serfs and slaves. Craftsmen and traders had lower status. Lower still were labourers. The Industrial Revolution created a new class of bankers and businessmen and factory workers and clerks and corporate executives. Social mobility became possible. Still, society continues to be dominated by the educated (Brahmins) and the powerful (Kshatriyas) and the rich (Vaishyas), not the disempowered service-provider (Shudra), which seems like a politically correct word for servant. It is so in India, it is so elsewhere.

15

Is yoga a Hindu concept?

In America, the question of whether yoga is a Hindu concept has been raised because of politics and economics. Some Hindus argue that yoga has been appropriated by the West, and made commercial, hence corrupt, and stripped of its spiritual significance. Western academicians argue, that yoga never belonged to Hindus and so the question of appropriation does not arise. Essentially it has become a territorial fight about is it 'yours' or is it 'mine', the very 'knots' that yoga seeks to unravel.

There is no doubt that the idea originated in the Indian subcontinent (referred to as South Asia nowadays in academic circles) over hundreds of years. The form that we know it in today is the result of the 'repackaging' that happened in the early twentieth century, done in India by Hindus, especially those who lived in the erstwhile Mysore state.

Indus valley seals show a man seated in a posture that is known in yoga as bhadrasana, or the throne position. Was this yoga? We can speculate either way.

Vedic traditions that are 4000 years old refer to the word 'yoga' in the sense of yoking or harnessing a cow to a cart. Even today, yoga, or its colloquial form 'jog', is used to indicate the alignment of various forces, such as the planetary forces in astrology. One can argue that the word 'jugaad' comes from 'jogi', the resourceful man who can create 'jog' where none existed before. So, the word has Vedic roots.

The shramana, or hermit, traditions, that are 3000 years old, bring forth many ideas that came to be seen as yogic. Ideas such as psychological discipline, focusing (dhyan) and building awareness or perspective (dharana), or withdrawing (pratyahara), and a whole bunch of breathing exercises (pranayama) to regulate the mind and physical contortions (asana) such as standing on one foot, or holding the arms aloft, favoured by hermits known as tapasvins, who do tapasya, or the churning of spiritual fire known as tapa, that grants humans supernatural physical and psychological powers (siddhi) that enable them to control nature. So, the practices today associated with yoga do have roots in shramana tradition. Buddhism and Jainism are shramana traditions.

In the Puranic age, 2000 years ago, Vedic rituals and eventually shramana traditions, were overshadowed by the stories of God, manifesting as Shiva, Vishnu and Devi, who value the household over ascetic lifestyles. Shiva became the God who reveals Yoga to his student Patanjali, a serpent, who in turn shares it with the world. Vishnu also shares it, as Krishna, with Arjuna, and with Hanuman as Ram. Here, we start seeing a division. Some focus more on the psychological aspect, ideas such as the union of the individual soul (jiva-atma) with the cosmic soul (para-atma) that is God, which is known as samadhi. Others focus on the physical aspects, especially magical powers, related to celibacy, which is known as siddhi. Samadhi focus is believed to be Vedic and siddhi focus is Tantrik, though such divisions are arbitrary. The focus varies in various texts. In the Bhagavad Gita, which is part of the Mahabharata, for example, there is reference to the psychological aspect of yoga, and to pranayama, but not to asanas, while in Patanjali's yoga sutra, the reference to asanas is minimal, but it does give a clear definition of yoga (removal of mental twists and turns), and feels no obligation to be overly theistic, except functionally.

In the Nath traditions, which became increasingly popular 1000 years ago, there are clear references to the physical aspect of yoga: various yogic postures and breathing exercises. These are used by ash-smeared mendicants who revere Matsyendranath and Gorakhnath. The more radical members of this school of thought are the naked ascetics that fascinate the West, and satisfy their craving for the exotic.

Since the nineteenth century, during British rule, to counter the European discourse, and following the exposure to European-style gymnastics, under the patronage of the Wodeyar kings of Mysore, local gurus of traditional physical culture such as Krishnamacharya conceptualized and organized yoga as we know it today and it spread across India and around the world through teachers such as Iyengar and Sivananda. Translations of and commentaries on ancient and medieval yoga texts such as Patanjali's yoga sutra were propagated by scholars and academicians, including Vivekananda.

India has transformed from a geographic term used by the Greeks to a political term referring to the secular republic of India, while Indic is a cultural term. Hindu, once a geographical term used by Arabs and Persians, has now become a religious term. Depending on how good a lawyer you are, you can argue that yoga is Indian, or Indic, or Hindu.

Today the idea and practice of yoga has spread widely across the world, alarming on one hand Christian and Muslim isolationists and supremacists (who view this as covert Hindu missionary activity) and Hindu isolationists and supremacists (who fear appropriation of their faith and culture). Then there are the atheists and secularists, also seeking supremacy, who see red every time the word 'tradition' or 'religion' is mentioned.

We must be careful of arguments presented by Right wing and Left wing thinkers, both of whom are outliers in all cultures, but tend to dominate discourse and take away nuance. The Right wing, especially the Hindu supremacists among them, tend to believe that yoga emerged in its perfect pristine form within Hinduism somewhere in the distant past, even before the Indus valley civilization. The Left wing has contempt for all things ancient, religious or traditional. These two wings feed off each other as they spend all their time arguing against each other's ideas, rather than appreciating that history is neither simple nor linear.

To deny that yoga has no special relationship with India, with Hinduism, Buddhism and Jainism, is like saying America has nothing to do with Native Americans (except being built on their corpses). At the same time, to accuse the West of stealing yoga is unfair; ideas do transform following cultural exchange. The idea of 'purity' that many religious and academic folk cling to is dangerous as it ultimately ends up establishing 'untouchability'.

Therefore, to answer the question, one needs to agree that yoga is Hindu. But more appropriately, it is Indic, for the idea was also developed by Buddhists, Jains, and a whole bunch of people who lived in the Indian subcontinent. And now it is becoming global.

Customs

16

Why are Hindus so ritualistic?

Hinduism is ritualistic. But rituals are not unique to Hinduism. All humans are ritualistic.

Ritual is essentially language, a way of communicating through formal choreographed gestures. It features significantly in Hinduism. There is the Vedic yagna, when formless celestial deities are invoked. There is the Agamic puja, where divinity is seen in an icon that is treated as a guest – invited, bathed, clothed, fed and adored. There is the sanskara or rites of passage like marriage, birth and death. There is the utsava or festivals celebrated annually. There are vrata or disciplines observed on particular days. Some are obligatory, some are voluntary. Some rituals are fixed by the movements of the sun and the moon and others are unplanned. Rituals are full of colour and fragrance, gestures and songs, stories and performances, food and music and clothes. They make Hinduism visible. Without them there is no Hinduism to see or hear or smell or touch or taste.

Ritual is one the three ways in which a culture transmits ideas over generations, the other two being story and symbol. The transmission of ritual is often separated from its understanding. Whether it makes sense to you or not, you are obliged to perform the ritual for the benefit of future generations who may see the sense of it. At a sheer mechanical level, even without any understanding, a ritual binds us to a community. For example, the ritual of namaaz binds the entire Muslim community. Whether a ritual makes sense or not, whether the arguments provided by people about its origin and meaning appeal to the rational mind or not, the simple act of performing it identifies the individual as part of a community.

Rituals can be religious or secular. For example, a puja is a religious ritual. A birthday party is a secular ritual. Both have a set of rules that have to be followed. Sometimes the rules are rigid, for example, the way a Catholic priest conducts Sunday Mass is determined by the Roman papacy, and the way the birthdays of employees are celebrated is determined by a corporate HR department.

In the nineteenth century, in an attempt to make Hindus defensive, orientalists came up with the idea that religious folk are primitive and excessively ritualistic while educated folk shun rituals. Ritual was attributed to ideas like God. The word 'ritual' was not used for various choreographed public performances designed to evoke faith in secular ideas like the state. Think of an Independence Day parade; it is no different from a jayanti celebration. Both contribute to the creation of communities, secular or religious. The former evokes patriotism and the latter evokes devotion.

In Vedic times, performing a yagna was considered karma and dharma. Later, the words 'karma' and 'dharma' came to be applied to social activities. As a result, marriage, childbirth and funeral were made ritualistic, obligatory, binding man to a larger community, which included his ancestors and even the gods.

A ritual can be seen as performance art. Like art, it communicates viscerally, through the body, and not through the spoken word. You sense it. You feel it. Wisdom rushes into the body via sensory organs and by evoking emotion. You can witness it – like witnessing a puja. You can participate in it – like participating in a puja. But if you view it as a tourist, with detachment, it will not evoke the response it evokes in someone who lets the art overtake him. The same happens in a museum: some people respond to the art, because they open themselves to the art, while others don't see the point.

Rituals also perform the important function of filling the time, so that the mind is distracted with activity and not bored. This is why communities create daily, weekly and annual prayers and festivals that everyone is expected to participate in. The obligation structures the time of the family and the community. It creates a repetitive rhythm. For Hindus, the procession of festivals binds the community together and marks the march of time, and enables you to look forward to something. So, if the time before the rains is marked with Shivaratri and Holi, the time after the rains is marked with Diwali and Dussehra.

Rituals can be overwhelming and repressive when they are based on obligation and not free will. For people who are independent minded, this can be a torture. Some people avoid them and some revel in them. For those people who need to be part of an ecosystem, rituals play a key role in making them a member of a social group – a family, a caste, a tribe, a company. If we are human, if we want to connect humans in a community, if we want to feel that life has a design and predictability, we need rituals.

17

Why do Hindus worship idols?

 The tension between giving God form and stripping God of any form is an ancient one. But what needs to be questioned is who made the rules that direct how Hindus, or anybody for that matter, should worship the divine. From where did this idea of frowning upon the ancient practice of idol worship come?

Abrahamic myth frowns upon any attempts to give God form, and the Bible condemns idolatry as indicative of a false religion.

The Muslim rulers of India frowned upon the practice of idol worship. Their raids on temples, which were conducted mainly for political reasons and economic gain (temples were repositories of great wealth), were justified by stating they were an exercise against infidel idolatry. The influence of Islam led many Hindus to prefer the formless divine (nirguni,

N.B.

nirakar) to divinity with form (saguni, sakar). So, we find some bhakti followers using the name of God to refer to an abstract entity, while others use the name of Ram or Krishna or Kali to refer to an unambiguous deity.

In the nineteenth century, as the British became masters of India, Hindus were pressured to defend the practice of idol worship. And so many Hindu reformers went to the extent of saying 'true' Hinduism, in its pristine form (by which they meant the Vedas), had no idols. That idol worship was a later-day corruption. However, many Hindu traditionalists rejected this idea.

Idolatry refers to taking things literally rather than metaphorically, focusing less on the idea and meaning that is formless rather than the word or symbol which is the form. An idea can be communicated only using a form (word, symbol, story, ritual). However, when the vehicle becomes more important than the content, when the form becomes more important than the idea, idolatry starts. We need idols (word, symbol, story, ritual) for sake of communication. But we need to differentiate between the vehicle and the content. Every civilization crumbles when the vehicle is taken literally at the cost of content. Those who take the vehicle literally are called fundamentalists; they do not bother with the underlying idea. So, they see the idol as God, rather than as a concrete expression of the idea of God.

For example, every year, in Mumbai, people bring clay images of Ganesha home, and worship him for a few days, before immersing the image in the sea. The ritual makes one aware of the transitory nature of life – even god comes and goes, is created and destroyed. The ritual involves veneration (aradhana) – welcoming the divine, bathing them, offering them food, clothes, perfumes, lamps, incense, and finally words of praise, before bidding them farewell. Thus, divinity is seen as an important guest, and treated as one. The act involves concentration (dhyana). During the festival, the name of Ganesha is chanted and his stories told so that our mind is filled with ideas about life, death, existence, wealth, power, impermanence, relationships, sorrow, liberation, success, pleasure. We express our desires and hope these will be fulfilled by the deity. Thus, we are connected to a force larger than ourselves. At the same time, the ritual involves engaging with friends, and family, and creating a sense of auspiciousness (mangalya) that generates positive energy in the house. We realize how fragile life is and how lucky we are to have a good life. We are asked to gaze upon the image (darshan) so that we recognize in the elephant head and corpulent body the forces of earth that generate wealth and power, and how they are all impermanent, how even the hermit Shiva has to become a householder for the benefit of humanity at large. Thus, the ritual anchored by the idol harnesses the Hindu idea and helps us reconnect with Hindu-ness, a shift from our otherwise mundane material life, a moment to pause about existence and our role in the cosmos.

The outsider will see this ritual as 'idolatry'. All rituals and prayers, of all religions, eventually seem like idolatry to the outsider, whether it is bowing to the image of Jesus nailed to a crucifix, or going around the Kabaa in Mecca, or singing before the menorah, or carrying the Granth Sahib in a palanquin, or dancing to the beat of a tribal drum ritual in the forest. But the insider, who is immersed in the ritual, engages with the larger ideas of life and existence through the tangible vehicles created by his ancestors.

In the Vedas, gods were embodied through chants (mantra). There was no material form. The only form was sound. As Vedic ideas spread, they mingled with the local faith of people who venerated the earth's fertility in the form of serpent-spirits (naga) and tree-spirits (yaksha) as well as gods (bhuta, deva) who lived in water bodies, mountains, rocks and caves. The earliest temples were groves, or rocks by a river, or a mountain peak. Later, pillars were erected to mark a deity. Then images were carved on stone or clay or metal. The gods began to look more and more like humans, but sometimes with multiple heads and hands, sometimes part animal, sometimes part bird. Imagination congealed into imagery. In the Agama literature, detailed instructions are given on how to establish an idol in a temple and transform it into a deity through rituals known as breath-establishing (prana-pratishtha). These are vehicles of faith. Contained in the image and the ritual and the accompanying story, is the idea that helps man discover the infinity described in the Vedas. It helps him bring the divine into his life.

Abrahamic faiths are uncomfortable with idols and images. Catholicism is the only exception where God is visualized as an old man and there is much art to show heaven, hell, prophets, angels and demons. However, Protestants shunned such art. Muslims are forbidden to show images of the Prophet though some artists in medieval Persia tried (while keeping him veiled) but the human desire to express divinity through art has not been crushed. Instead of human forms, Islamic artists used calligraphy and architecture to express the divine spirit. Others have used music to give the formless form. Hinduism has no restrictions – divinity is expressed through nature, through artefacts, through trees and animals and humans and fantastic creatures.

Abrahamic religions fear human imagination and tend to restrict it using rules and bans against art. This tendency to control human imagination and the ultimate manifestation of the divine is slowly creeping into Hinduism with fundamentalism and attacks on artists. Anyone who seeks to control expressions of divinity seeks to contain divinity. Hinduism venerates human imagination. The wise Hindu sages knew that the divine is infinite potential and has innumerable expressions. We can access the limitless through limitations of artificial and natural forms – by using icons of Ram and Krishna and Durga and Ganesha, that the ignorant condescendingly refer to as idolatry.

18

Do Hindus worship the phallus?

 o Christians worship dead bodies and torture instruments since images of a dead Jesus nailed to a cross, or the cross itself, which was a Roman torture instrument, are found in every Church? Every Catholic sees these as images of the saviour who died for his or her sins. A non-Catholic sees something else. Who is correct? The believer, or the non-believer?

Most Hindus do not see the Shiva-linga as a phallus. However, some academicians do. Whose view is correct? To understand the mystery of the Shiva-linga, we must appreciate the difference between a symbol and a sign. A symbol has multiple meanings but a sign has a single meaning. A symbol's meaning depends on context and needs to be understood in the context of ritual and story as well as by comparing and contrasting it with other symbols that may complement or contrast it.

In Hinduism, two concepts are very powerful: yonija and ayonija. Yoni means womb. Yonija means one born of a womb. Such a creature has a past life: it is the fruit of a seed. Ayonija means one not born of a womb. Such a creature does not have a past life: it is not the fruit of a seed. It is self-born, swayambhu. Yonija are part of the sansara and the karmic cycle: they take birth and they die, bound by rules of space and time. Ayonija or swayambhu are not part of the sansara or the karmic cycle: they exist always, unbound by the rules of space and time.

The Shiva-linga is a representation of that swayambhu. The dripping water-pot above the Shiva-linga and the trough around it that collects the water embodies the yoni-patra or Shakti-pitha, the seat of the goddess, the world of birth and death. Thus, the Shiva temple symbolically communicates the two fundamental principles of Hinduism: the time-bound recurring world of matter (prakriti, shakti, maya) and the timeless still world of the soul (purusha, shiva, brahman). These ideas are found in the Vedas, elaborated in the Upanishads and given shape and form in the Puranas, the Tantras and the Agamas.

Phallic worship is common in many mythologies. And it is typically associated with fecundity (more children, more crops, more cattle). It is also used to ward away troublesome spirits, frighten them, very much in the way many people use sexual swear words involving the penis. In ancient Egypt, Min was a fertility god depicted with an erect phallus. In ancient Greece, images of Hermes and Pan with erect phalluses were used as boundary markers in farms. Even today, if you travel to Bhutan, you will find penis statues being sold as good luck charms and warders of bad luck on the street.

Hindus worship the Shiva-linga. In many Puranas, the Shiva-linga is described as the erect penis of Shiva. The worship of the Shiva-linga, especially on Mondays, is popular among young unmarried girls searching for husbands. Shiva is said to be the source of the Kama Sutra and in the Kumarasambhavam, Kalidasa's Sanskrit poem on the birth of Shiva's son, he is rather erotic. So, it is easy to jump to the conclusion that Hindus worship the phallus and Shiva is an erotic god. What makes Shiva mysterious is that he is also the great ascetic, associated with celibacy and continence. This dual personality makes him mysterious. For the West — conditioned by an unmarried Jesus, a virginal Mary, and a God who has no consort — this image of a god who is erotic and visualized allegedly as a phallus can be quite titillating. But it reveals a rather superficial understanding of the symbol that is not aligned to the larger Hindu philosophies.

But the idea of the Shiva-linga has nothing to do with fertility. In fact, Shiva is called the 'destroyer'. We must ask the question: why did Hindus choose to visualize a 'destroyer' using a 'phallic' symbol which is traditionally used for fertility? To qualify Shiva as a fertility god reveals an inability to grasp refined philosophies.

Traditionally, Hinduism has two paths: the outward path (pravritti) and the inward path (nivritti). The outward path belongs to the householder and the inward path belongs to the hermit. The householder marries and the hermit does not. The householder sheds his semen in the womb – the womb being both literal (of his wife) and symbolic (of his society). Thus, he creates. The hermit does not marry and through the practice of celibacy and tapasya does not shed his semen. In fact he 'reverses the flow of semen' according to Tantrik texts, which is called urdhva-retas, symbolized as a hermit with erect phallus but eyes closed. So, he is aroused but not by external sensory stimuli but by inner wisdom and power. Shiva is the hermit who is being encouraged by the Goddess to participate in the household. Hence, the Shiva Purana describes his marriage to Sati and Parvati, and his tryst with Ganga, and the birth of his sons, Kartikeya (Murugan in Tamil Nadu) and Ganesha. This idea is presented in the Shiva-linga with its yoni-patra.

Monday is associated with the moon, the graha (celestial body in astrology) associated with emotions and love. Unmarried girls worship the Shiva-linga, on Mondays, hoping that like Parvati they too will be able to transform a hermit into a householder, and get a good husband, one who is as considerate, devoted and compassionate as Shiva.

The world of Shakti is the world of nama (name) and rupa (form). Shiva is outside both name and form. He embodies atma, and so has no one characteristic. He is formless or nirguna. How does one revere the formless? To do so, a rishi of yore either just picked up a river stone, shaped by the flowing water (a symbol of time), and worshipped it by placing it erect in the ground, or simply creating a mound of sand on the riverbank. This became the Shiva-pinda or the Shiva-linga, the form of the formless, the linga of the a-linga. This is what the believer sees. And that is all that matters.

19

Why do Hindus light lamps?

It is curious that the practice of lighting lamps, which seems integral to Hinduism today, is not a practice with Vedic roots, indicating its entry into Puranic Hinduism from non-Vedic Hinduism, a subject on which we have little information.

A key feature of Hinduism, whether Vedic or Puranic, is the invocation of a god or a goddess (avahan), inviting him or her for a meal (bhog) and asking him or her for a blessing after he or she has been fed (phalastuti), and then bidding him or her farewell (visarjan).

In Vedic Hinduism, this was done through burning wood placed in a fire-pit made of bricks. The fire was Agni, mouth of the gods. Food was offered in the form of ghee (clarified butter) made potent by the chant of mantras (formulae). This was perhaps the practice of common folk in India who worshipped trees and rocks and rivers and mountains, the various yakshas and nagas, using these rituals.

But in later Puranic Hinduism, that arose 2000 years ago, the gods are no longer abstract entities. They become icons and offerings become very understandable: bath (abhishek), clothes (vastra), food (naivedya), unguents (gandha), incense (dhoop) and lamp (deep). Here, fire is admired not for its ability to consume ghee, or generate heat, but for its ability to bring light. In the evening people were encouraged to light a lamp so that travellers could find a refuge. Even today, people are asked to light lamps in the evening and place them near the doorway to help people find their way.

A lamp indicated the presence of a potter who made the clay lamp, or the affluent who could afford a metal lamp, the oil presser who provided the oil, or a cowherd who provided ghee, a farmer who provided the cotton wick. In other words, the lamp was a symbol of culture (sanskriti) and lighting it indicated both abundance and consideration. Grand temples lit with lamps placed on their vast roofs revealed the majesty of the local deity and king. In Maharashtra, one finds specially designed pillars bearing hundreds of stone lamps that are lit during festivals to recreate the pillar of fire through which Shiva appeared before the world. In art, gods are shown holding fire in their palms or their hair appearing as flames.

The lamp was lit by housewives primarily and is very different from the fire in the yagnashala lit by Brahmins, which in turn is very different from the campfire (dhuni) of sanyasis. The campfire has no container (vedi) of bricks, revealing its wild nature. The fire of the yagnashala indicated domestication. The lamp signified a shift from the public to the private, the rise of a more settled agrarian rural lifestyle of later Hindus as against the nomadic lifestyle of early Hindus, or Vedic people.

Philosophically, humans are the only animals that control fire. So, the journey from dhuni to yagnashala agni to deep-lakshmi reveals the increased cultivation of culture. It is also a journey to affluence and abundance. Thus, lighting lamps was an indicator of wealth and power. More lamps naturally indicated more prosperity. So, they were lit regularly during celebrations. There were lamps on the walls of houses. They were put on boats to float in ponds and rivers during various festivals. They were placed in the sky (kandil, or akash deep) using lanterns. Lamps are lit during Diwali to mark the end of the monsoons and the start of a new year. With lamps, the gods are invited into the house, the foremost being Ram, the responsible sage-king, and Lakshmi, the goddess of fortune.

Fire, therefore, plays a fundamental role in mythology. It embodies hunger that consumes, heat that comforts, and wisdom that enlightens.

20

Is a Hindu prayer different from a Christian or Muslim one?

Hindu prayers are very different from Christian and Muslim prayers, and, also, from Sikh, Buddhist and Jain prayers. Prayers exist in a mythic worldview, and depending on the worldview, the nature of the prayer is different.

For example, Buddhists and Jains do not believe in the concept of a single all-powerful God that is found in Islam, Christianity and Sikhism, so naturally a Buddhist prayer is bound to be different from a Muslim, Christian or Sikh one. Christians, Muslims and Sikhs believe in an all-powerful singular formless God. The purpose of their prayers is to acknowledge this God and experience humility before God's greatness and grandeur.

In Christians, there is an additional purpose – to ask for forgiveness for their sins, a concept not found in Islam.

In Islam, prayer is reinforcing the article of faith that God is great and there is no God but God (Allah in Arabic). Everything happens because of Allah. In Sikhism, the prayer acknowledges that the formless singular God treats all creature equally, thus alluding to the social inequality that is part of Hindu faith. The Sikhs also acknowledge their Gurus just as Muslims acknowledge the Prophet and Christians acknowledge Jesus as the son of God who leads one towards God.

In these prayers, there is a sense of consistency and homogeneity, as everyone is part of a single faith, and there is one way of praying. No innovations are allowed. The church, mosque and gurudwara are places where the faithful gather, and everyone, all together, prays in the same way, using the same prayers and same rituals. This evokes a sense of equality before God, and humility before a powerful force.

In Buddhism, prayers are not offered to any deity. They are meant to help the mind focus and concentrate, and make the journey towards either mindlessness or mindfulness. Here prayer is part of the meditative process that is central to Buddhism. In some Buddhist schools, one does pray to the Adi Buddha, or the eternal Buddha, who lives in the pure land of Sukhavati, and watches over all humanity as Avatilokeshwara Bodhisattva, or to the Buddha-chitta within all human beings. Thus, there is an object of prayer, who is the wise teacher, or the wisdom possibility, but not God.

In Jainism, prayers are offered to the great sages, teachers, gurus and deities, who enable the Jain in his personal journey of purification. Every individual prays in his individual way, based on prescribed techniques and rituals. There are special prayers where the holy men of yore, such as arhats and tirthankaras, are celebrated and their glory acknowledged. There is, however, no all-powerful God here who controls one destiny or makes rules about the world. The gods and gurus enshrined in temples are those who help us negotiate our way through this world that is an impersonal infinite and eternal entity functioning with its own rules.

Some Hindus will say the act of praying is good enough. This is karma yoga. Others will say that the emotion accompanying the prayer is more important than the prayer. This is bhakti yoga. Some will say that the meaning of the words of the prayer are important and they reveal the truth of the universe. This is gyan yoga.

The purpose of the Hindu prayer is to invoke the deity (avahan), praise them (aarti), and eventually ask for their help (phalastuti). The gods are addressed in very personal terms – their form is described, their attributes admired, their adventures recounted. The prayer seems like a petition, almost transactional, for after praising the deity for helping so many in distress, the devotee asks for both psychological well-being as well as the solution to his or her problems. In Hindu prayers, there is no concept of confession, though a devotee can seek forgiveness from a deity if he wants to, to allay his guilt and shame, but that does not guarantee escape from what is written in his karma. Prayers can be made to various forces like planets and directions to improve living conditions and to ward away malevolent forces.

Different gods are called upon for different purposes and different occasions – Saraswati is favoured in schools, Lakshmi in businesses, Durga by politicians. The same devotee can pray to different gods at different times, in different moods, as per his need. There is no obsession with monotheism. Depending on comfort, every deity is seen as different, and every deity is seen as a manifestation of the same divine. Prayers to village or family gods create a sense of community, but may not be appreciated by people from outside the village or family or clan. Prayers and rituals of the Vaishnava Brahmins of Tamil Nadu may be very different from the prayers and rituals of the Vaishnava Brahmins of the Gangetic plains. Prayers that were popular in Vedic times have given way to prayers that are more popular with the masses, like the Hanuman Chalisa in the local dialect of Hindi.

Some prayers are meant for temples, some for household shrines, some can be offered anywhere and anytime. Some can be long elaborate hymns with correct pronunciation and melody. Some require just chanting a hymn or the god's name repeatedly. Some prayers are part of rituals, some are not. Some are meant for the deity outside. Some are meant to calm one's mind, said to be the deity inside our body-temple. Regular household prayers have long been used by parents to educate their children in the ways of culture. Bhajans and kirtans became popular during the freedom struggle to create community groups across religious sects and castes. Thus, prayers are highly customized to individual needs, though strongly influenced by family and other social forces.

Hindu prayer is marked by diversity. There are Vedic prayers and Agamic prayers, prayers in Sanskrit and prayers in regional languages. There are prayers with only rituals and no words. There are communal bhajans and kirtans and there are private prayers chanted only by priests in temples, not the uninitiated. There are prayers for Shiva, for Vishnu, for Ram and Krishna, for Durga and Saraswati. This multi-faceted, different and dynamic approach to prayer, where you can substitute one for the other, is unique to Hinduism.

21

Is the Hindu thread ceremony the same as the Christian baptism?

Baptism is a Christian ritual by which one declares their acceptance of Jesus Christ as the son of God, and humanity's deliverer. In other words, baptism marks one's admission into the Christian church; unless baptized, one cannot not be a Christian. Likewise, until a man undergoes circumcision, he cannot be Jewish, or Muslim. These are ritual declarations of one's covenant, or agreement, with God. This idea of making a contract with God and becoming a member of the faith by a ritual is alien to Hinduism. One becomes Hindu by birth.

The thread ceremony is known by various names in different parts of India: Upanayanam in south India, Brata ghara ritual in Odisha, Janayu in Gujarat, Munja in Maharashtra and Karnataka, Poita in Bengal. But what is it? It depends on who you ask.

Historically, the thread ceremony is linked to Vedic Aryans. We find a similar ceremony among Parsis, who are an offshoot of the Indo-Iranian branch of Vedic Aryans. In an elaborate Navjote ceremony, the thread of seventy-two fibres (representing seventy-two chapters of the sacred text) is wrapped around the waist of the boy or girl three times and knotted in the front and the back. The untying and retying is done by the faithful to the chanting of prayers several times a day. Like a baptism, this ceremony, marks a person's entry into the Zoroastrian faith which thrived in Iran (ancient Persia) before the rise of Islam. Though linked to Vedic roots, Zoroastrian faith is highly linear in structure (one life) in contrast to the Vedic faiths that are cyclical in structure (many lives).

In Vedic times, there was probably no thread. Instead a garment was worn over the left shoulder during household rituals and right shoulder during funeral rituals. Some Brahmins used deer skin as the upper garment and the spot where the head of the deer was located is today indicated by the Brahma-granthi knot. This is speculation, of course, but what scholars are confident of is that the 'thread' became a key part of the Hindu dress code in medieval and modern times, as the caste system became increasingly rigid and draconian.

In the dharma-shastras, there is reference to a sacred thread ceremony for men and women, and members of all varnas, not just Brahmins. In art, we find gods and goddesses sporting the sacred thread over their left shoulder. The thread is sometimes bejewelled, revealing they are all twice-born, with access to Vedic wisdom. However, by medieval times, this became a singular ritual to identify the Brahmin male, and locate him on top of the Hindu caste pyramid.

The ritual involves the placement of nine cotton fibres, twisted to make three threads, and knotted as one and worn over the left shoulder.

The nine individual fibres embody the sound Om, fire (Agni), serpent (Naga), moon (Soma), ancestors (pitr), the gods of birth (Prajapati), breath (Vayu), death (Yama) and the world (Vishwadeva). When bunched as three, they represent the three gods (Brahma, Vishnu, Shiva), the three goddesses (Lakshmi, Durga, Saraswati), three forms of the goddess of learning (Gayatri, Savitri, Sharada or Saraswati), the three primary Vedas (Rig, Sama, Yajur), the three primary shastras (dharma-shastra, artha-shastra, kama-shastra), the three yogas (gyan, bhakti, karma), the three Vedic fires (for the household or grahapatya, for death or dakshinagni, for the gods or avahaniya). The single knot is Brahma-granthi, which embodies infinity (ananta). Thus, symbolically, the thread embodies Vedic wisdom.

The threads are kept pure, hooked over the right ear during urination and defecation, and replaced annually. During funeral ceremonies, the threads are hung over the right shoulder. Some Brahmins wear these threads from childhood, throughout their life, while others wear it only while performing Vedic rituals, like marriage and funeral ceremonies.

Today conservatives still see the thread ceremony as a particularly Brahmin male ritual, upholding the caste structure.

The not-so-conservative see this is a ritual for all children being initiated into the Vedic fold, irrespective of gender and caste. At the conventional end of the spectrum, also, a thread ceremony is a ritual limited to Brahmin males that grants them a guru who will reveal to them the secrets of the Vedas. The liberals see this as just a ritual that marks the child's entry into formal schooling, where he or she prepares for the life ahead. They expand the narrow definition of the Vedas to include all knowledge, formal and informal, material and spiritual. It becomes a rite of passage that embarks any person, boy or girl, of any caste, on the path of learning and education. The thread ceremony makes you a dvija, or twice-born.

The first birth of humans takes place physically via the mother's womb. The second birth is psychological, via the guru's teaching of the Vedas. After the sacred thread ceremony, the child is ready to go to school and receive education. He, or she, is trained through various practices and teachings to expand (brah-) his or her mind (manas) and so discover the Brahman. This was the original meaning of the word Brahmin, he who expands the mind and seeks the infinite Brahman.

Considering these perspectives, then, the thread ceremony is not the same as baptism.

22

Why do Hindus prefer celebrating birth anniversaries over death anniversaries?

Hindus prefer celebrating joyful birth anniversaries (jayanti) over mournful death anniversaries (punya tithi). The reason for this is that Hindus regard birth as auspicious and death as inauspicious. Death of demons (asuras and rakshasas) are seen triumphs of gods, heralding peace and prosperity, hence celebrated.

The Ramayana is more sacred than the Mahabharata, because the former describes the birth of Ram, while the latter does not describe the birth of Krishna. More value is placed on the Bhagavata Purana where Krishna's birth is described. Further, most Hindu festivals are about the birth of a God (Ram's birth, Krishna's birth, Hanuman's birth, Garuda's birth) or about the death of a demon (killing of Mahisha by Durga, killing of Ravana by Ram, killing of Naraka by Krishna).

121

This is rather different from the Christian practice of mourning the death of Jesus Christ (Good Friday), and observing the martyrdom of saints, or the Shia Muslim practice of lamenting the death of the Prophet's son-in-law's family (Muharram). The mourning of Imam Hussain continues in Shia Islam even today, 1400 years after the event. The crucifixion of Jesus Christ is enacted by many communities even after 2000 years. In Hinduism, however, Shiva, known as 'Smarantaka' and 'Yamantaka', is the destroyer of memory and death; he liberates us, makes us step out of history, and discover the timeless soul.

All religions have something like All Soul's Day where the living remember the dead. In Hinduism, this is the fortnight of Pitr Paksha when rituals are performed for the dead. But there is a difference. The dead in Christianity and Islam are in purgatory, having lived their lives in full, waiting for the Day of Judgement. The dead in Hinduism are waiting for rebirth. But by and large, association with death is shunned in Hindu traditions, especially when compared with the value placed on death in other religions.

In Islamic and Christian traditions, death is valued and so tombs and graves become monuments. Traditionally, in most Hindu communities, no relics of the dead were kept in or around the house. All things that touch death were seen as polluting and inauspicious. In later Hindu monastic tradition, the bodies of dead teachers were buried and a tulsi plant grown above the grave. Though it is not worshipped, the place of burial is thus marked. They are buried and not cremated as it is believed that they have attained samadhi and will not be reborn; this renders their last inhabited body auspicious. This Hindu practice may have come from Buddhists who kept relics (tooth, hair, bones) of great teachers, after their cremation.

When Muslim kings started building tombs for their predecessors, many Hindu kings also demanded that pavilions and 'chhattris' be built to mark the spot where a former king was cremated. We find this practice in Rajasthan, for example. This practice continues in modern times, with tombs being built to mark the cremation spot of leaders who were Hindu, as in case of Mahatma Gandhi and Indira Gandhi. Burial to mark the dead is a practice followed by many Hindu communities who reject Brahminism and caste. Jayalalitha, who led one of the Dravida movements, was buried instead of cremated.

In Hinduism, the memory of death prevents progress, wisdom and liberation. It holds you down. The fear of death creates all mental modifications that can only be unravelled by yoga. Death and the fear of death are seen as entrapping. So, after a funeral, one is advised not to turn back and look at the crematorium. The past has to be forgotten. Hence, Hindus place greater value on mythological narratives than historical narratives as compared to other religions.

Nowadays, as the world craves vengeance in the name of 'justice', remembering past ills has become a powerful political tool. It helps rally mobs and bind people. For example, by referring to colonial rule, many nation states claim moral superiority and political mileage. War memorials are built to remind people not just about martyrs but also enemies of the nation state. The Dalit movement keeps speaking of Brahmin hegemony that led to years of discrimination to mobilize 'lower' castes and tribes and Hindutva movement keeps speaking of '1000 years of enslavement' to rally Hindus against Muslims. Thus, the memory of the past, of death, of oppression, is used to shape the present.

Death can ensnare the living, it can prevent us from moving on and forward. Birth, rebirth, even double birth (via thread ceremony and accepting a guru) is seen as good and glorious. The auspicious direction is the east (purva) from where the sun rises. The auspicious orientation is the north (uttar) where stands the still and permanent Pole Star. The west (paschim), linked with sunset, and the south (dakshin), linked with death, are inauspicious. In the traditional Hindu scheme of things, it is better to forget the past (the West often mocks this as Hindu denial), and focus on the future. Past is death and death is bondage that denies us liberation (moksha).

23

Is divorce permitted in Hinduism?

 In many cultures, marriage is a contract. Divorce is a breaking of the contract. Some, like the Catholic church, believe that the contract of marriage is sacred and so must never be broken. Others disagree.

In Hinduism, marriage is not a contract. The Naradasmriti dharma-shastra (XII.97), a Hindu law book, states, 'When her husband is lost, or dead, becomes an ascetic, is impotent, or is expelled from caste, in these five conditions, a woman may remarry.' Katyayana adds that if the husband turns out to be of another caste, or the same gotra, or if he is guilty of foul acts, the wife may remarry. Do these verses suggest that divorce was allowed in Hinduism at some point?

Hindu marriage is a sanskara, or a rite of passage. Sanskara is that which gives shape (akara) to one's world (sansara) and helps one live a full life. The rituals include everything from shaving one's head as a child to feeding one solid food, educating one, repaying one's debts to one's ancestors and to society at large by getting one married and encouraging one to bear a child to enable those in the land of the dead to return to the land of the living, and by getting one to perform funeral rituals enabling the dead to move from the world of the living to the land of the ancestors.

Many Brahmins codified these rituals and rules over 1000 years in the dharma-shastras, from 200 BCE to 1200 CE. These rules were meant for 'upper' castes primarily, not for all. The general trend has been to forbid divorce, and allowing only widowers to remarry; women could not remarry even after widowhood.

We must keep in mind that Hinduism is an umbrella term and cannot be restricted only to 'upper' castes. In the epic tale of Nala and Damayanti, when the exiled nishadha-king Nala goes missing, Damayanti's father organizes a swayamvara so that she can find a new husband. In the Ramayana, Mandodari, widow of the rakshasa-king Ravana, marries her brother-in-law Vibhishana, and Tara, widow of the vanara-king Vali, marries Sugriva.

We must keep in mind that rules of marriage in Hinduism have changed over the centuries. In the Mahabharata, for example, Kunti informs Pandu of a time before marriage, when men and women chose each other freely. The sage Shvetaketu enforced the rules of marriage so that children could identify who their father was. He also allowed women of impotent men to bear children by other men, a practice known as niyoga. This is why even though Pandu's biological father is Vyasa, he is identified as the son of Vichitravirya. In the story of Oghavati, from the epic Mahabharata, the husband finds his wife in the arms of another man, and does not get upset, unlike the story of Ahalya, from the epic Ramayana, where Gautama curses his wife to turn to stone. Thus, these stories reveal shifting values over time.

The Bhagavata Purana tells us how Kardama marries Devahuti but abandons her after she bears him a son, Kapila. He is obliged to father a child so as to repay his debt to his ancestors. But he does not want to be a husband. He would rather be an ascetic. As does Jaratkaru who abandons his wife after the birth of his son. Then we hear stories of apsaras who agree to marry but leave their husbands who try to control them. Thus, Urvashi leaves Pururava and Ganga leaves Shantanu. Can we call this divorce?

While we are repeatedly told of demure housewives submitting to their husbands as per the Manusmriti, a trope repeated by pro-religion and anti-religion lobbies, few point to the stories in the Puranas where Goddesses get angry with their husbands and leave their homes, until their husbands appease them and beg them to come back. Lakshmi leaves Vaikuntha and Vishnu has to work hard to bring her back. Gauri leaves Kailasa and Shiva has to work hard to bring her back. These stories speak of the power and agency of the female characters, often denied to modern Hindu women, as everyone is cherry picking stories that fit the self-serving patriarchal framework.

In Vishnu temples, Lakshmi shrines are always separate from Vishnu's. In Dwarka, Rukmini stands separate from Krishna. In Pandharpur, Satyabhama stands in a shrine separate from Krishna. In this manner, she asserts her autonomy. Divorce, however, is not seen between the God and his consort. This is one reason why many Hindu couples perhaps prefer separation rather than legal divorce.

The Hindu marriage rite – sapta padi – where the couple takes seven steps to share seven worldly gifts is seen as an indissoluble bond. When things do not work out, the couple may physically separate, but is bound in spirit. It must be kept in mind that 'consent' does not play a role in Hindu marriage. Neither the boy nor the girl are asked if they want to marry, even though in the Puranas we hear of love marriage (gandharva vivah) and swayamvara (self-choice ceremony). These are seen an 'inferior' practices of primitive tribes, not suitable for 'upper' castes. Since marriage is not based on consent, the idea of divorce also makes no sense.

But these notions of a bond over several lifetimes are poetic and abstract. Hinduism has adjusted over history, geography and across communities to suit various requirements. In the parakiya bhakti tradition, Radha is described as another man's wife. The Atharva Veda describes the marriage of a woman called Surya to two gods, the Ashvins. The Puranas inform us of Marisha who marries ten Pracheta brothers. In Vaishnava temples, Lakshmi stands independent of the shape-shifting Vishnu, while in Shiva temples, Shakti embraces Shiva firmly despite a tempestuous marriage. In Chidambaram, Shiva dominates his wife but in Madurai, the Goddess dominates Shiva. All these instances reveal the vitality and variety in matters of marriage.

And so, it comes to pass that in the twenty-first century, Hinduism is well-found to allow notions of both separation and divorce.

24

Why do Hindus worship cows?

Hindus worship not only cows, but also cobras and monkeys and elephants. In Hinduism, divinity is visualized in various forms: elements, plants, animals, celestial bodies, artefacts, and geometrical forms. It is not uncommon for a Hindu to worship fire or water, the tulsi shrub or the banyan tree, the sun or the moon, a pot or a sword, a yantra made of intersecting triangles, circles and squares.

However, around the world, the image of Hindus worshipping the cow has captured the imagination of people, perhaps because in most parts of the world people eat beef, and they don't see cattle roaming the streets. Snakes and monkeys and elephants are eaten in many parts of the world, but not in Europe. Perhaps that is the reason the Hindu worship of these animals does not get as much attention.

While the cow is a sacred animal, the male cow or bull has been castrated for centuries in India, turned into a bullock and used to pull the plough or cart. In pastoral communities, a cow was useful as its milk provided nourishment and its dung served as fuel and plaster for the house and floor. Hence, cows were highly prized commodities. Taking care of cows and not harming cows is recommended in various Brahmin texts. Was this meant for all communities or only Brahmins? That is a matter of speculation. By 'cow' did they mean the milk-giving female or all species and genders of cattle? That is also a matter of speculation.

In Vedic times, a rishi-marriage was one where a man gave his daughter to a rishi, along with a cow and a bullock so that the couple would have a source of livelihood. A buffalo could serve the same purpose; however, it was clearly the cow that was given more importance.

In the Puranas, the cow came to be associated with Vishnu, while the uncastrated wild bull came to be associated with Shiva. Durga killed the male buffalo demon, while Ayyappa of Kerala kills the female buffalo demon.

In Vaishnava mythology, the cow came to be seen as the embodiment of Lakshmi, goddess of wealth. In the Bhagavata Purana, the earth takes the form of a cow and asks Vishnu to protect her. That is why Vishnu, her guardian, is called Go-pala, protector of the earth-cow. The earth is visualized as being milked by all living creatures. And when kings plunder earth's resources, they are described as cow killers, or cow tormenters, and Vishnu descends as Parashurama, Ram and Krishna, to kill the greedy kings and let the earth drink their blood.

Indra is said to have Kamadhenu, a wish-fulfilling cow, that rose from the ocean of milk. Rishi Vasistha had a similar cow and when Kaushika tried to steal it, the cow produced an army to protect itself. Rishi Jamadagni also had such a cow, and when Kartaviryarjuna tried to steal it, the rishi's son, Parashurama, hacked the king to pieces.

In the Raghuvamsa, we are told how Ram's ancestor Dilip shields a cow from being attacked by a lion and offers himself as food to the lion. This can be taken literally – save the cow even if it means killing yourself. Or it can be taken metaphorically – where culture (king) restrains its hunger so that cultivated and domesticated land (cow) does not encroach on the wild spaces (lion). This tension between destroying nature for the sake of culture is a major theme of kingship in India, and is described as a 'dharma-sankat', for dharma is essentially a reversal of jungle law, where the mighty protect, rather than feed on, the meek.

The image of Krishna as the lovable cowherd god probably originated in Tamil Sangam literature and became part of Sanskrit literature in the Harivamsa, the appendix of the Mahabharata that describes Krishna's childhood. In the Bhagavata Purana, Krishna kills a bull-demon called Arishtha and a calf-demon called Vatsa.

Hermit orders such as Buddhism and Jainism popularized ideas of compassion, non-violence and vegetarianism. They opposed Vedic rituals that at one time included animal sacrifices. In fact, according to Jayadeva, Vishnu descended as Buddha out of compassion for animals that were being killed as part of rituals.

However, Hinduism, unlike Buddhism and Jainism, has never been prescriptive. Castes and communities created rules for themselves, not for all. What was private was never public. As we have moved away from the caste structure to uniform civil structures, certain caste groups are imposing their private eating habits on the public, a phenomenon never seen before in India. The price of modernity, one can say.

Hinduism recognized that violence is integral to certain vocations like farming, animal husbandry and the leather industry. It saw culture as essentially violent – the destruction of forests was essential to establish fields, the castration of bulls and buffaloes was necessary for creating draught animals, and meat was a good source of food, especially in arid areas where animals helped turn inedible plants to into food. This balanced view is expressed in the Vyadha Gita of the Mahabharata where a butcher from Mithila transmits wisdom to a hermit! It drew attention to the idea that psychological violence can be as horrific as physical violence. And violence for food is not the same as violence for power.

In the last 1000 years, as first Islam and then the British came to India, Hinduism has become very fearful of contamination and obsessed with purification. Those who ate cows were seen as pollution, while cow urine and cow dung were seen as purifiers. This symbolic value made the cow a potent symbol of Hinduism, even more than old Puranic metaphors that equated cow with livelihood and the earth.

Increasingly, we find posters depicting all gods inside a cow. Thus worshipping a cow becomes equal to worshipping all Hindu gods. This makes the cow sacred. But there are also images of all the gods inside a tree, or inside a human. However, these have not acquired the same level of attention. These images mean to show that all gods are present in all creatures. That divinity is present in all things. However, the idea that all gods are present *only* inside a cow has been amplified so that eating a cow becomes equal to attacking Hindu gods. This powerful and popular code is now being used as a political tool to garner Hindu votes.

25

Are Hindus vegetarian?

Not all Hindus are vegetarian. As a matter of fact, most of them are not. Many Hindu and Jain immigrants in the USA and the UK spread the idea of a 'vegetarian' diet throughout the world. People assumed this applies to all Indians. One must also give due credit to the popularity of yoga, where vegetarian food is considered sattvic (creating calmness) while meat is considered rajasic (creating excitement). Being vegetarian distinguishes Hindus from other communities. It was viewed as being 'quaint' in Western societies, and over time, it has become the defining trait of Hinduism, regardless of any statistical support.

Hindus can be vegetarian and non-vegetarian. Hinduism is a plural religion, an umbrella term for many jatis, sampradayas and paramparas, some of whom may be vegetarian for some time, or not at all. There is no Hindu commandment telling Hindus what to eat or not to eat. This obsession with reducing Hinduism to a single behaviour is common among two factions of people: belligerent Hindutva radicals and their counterparts, the Hinduphobes.

Different communities in India have different food habits. And there is no one rule. For example, many people think all Brahmins are vegetarian. That is fiction. In south India, Brahmins are vegetarian. Highly educated, well-versed in mathematics, they migrated early to urban centres across India as accountants, journalists and bureaucrats. Exposure to them created the classical 'Madrasi' stereotype in Bollywood films, the man who eats only vegetarian food. This eclipses the vast non-vegetarian traditions of south India. Further, in Bengal, Brahmins eat fish, they also sacrifice goats and buffalo to the Goddess Kali as part of the Shakto tradition. In Kashmir, some Brahmin communities offer meat to Bhairava, a form of Shiva.

The story of a Tamil saint reveals Hindu attitudes towards food. Two kinds of devotees visited a Shiva temple: a vegetarian priest who followed all the rituals and a tribal hunter who did not know any rituals. Every dawn, the priest would perform the rituals as prescribed by the scriptures. At dusk, the hunter would reach the temple and give the deity there all that he had found in the forest that day: flowers, water from mountain springs and the best portion of the game he had hunted that day. He carried the flowers in his hair, and the water in his mouth (which he spat out). The game he would chew to make it tender and then offer it to the deity. The next dawn, the priest would find the meat, the bones and the dried flowers inside the temple and would be repulsed. This cycle continued for weeks. On Mount Kailasa, Shakti asked Shiva who was the favoured devotee?

Shiva decided to test the priest and the hunter. The Shiva-linga in the temple sprouted eyes. When the priest saw this, he felt it was a sign of divine blessings. But then one of the eyes started to bleed. Thinking this to be bad luck or a sign of divine rage, the priest ran away. The hunter, however, on seeing the bleeding eye, tried to heal it using forest herbs. Unable to stop the bleeding, he decided to cut out one of his eyes and give it to the deity. That stopped the bleeding in one eye, but then the other eye started to bleed. So, the hunter decided to cut out his other eye as well. But that would make him blind and he would not know where to heal the deity. To mark the spot, he put his foot on the bleeding eye. Just as he was about to blind himself, Shiva appeared and stopped him.

Through this fantastic story, we are asked to analyse what matters to the divine: our underlying emotion, or our ritual behaviour? God does not care about social hierarchies, our ritual notions of purity and contamination. God only cares about the human ability to love: the ability to overcome our own insecurities to take care of others in pain. Our aham (ego) makes us think we are purer and superior to others. The journey to atma makes us think that no one is impure or inferior, that everyone is worthy of respect. What matters is not the ritual worship of the priest, but the love of the hunter. Rituals need to be an expression of love, not a mechanistic practice, or a tool to indulge the ego by dominating others.

Some of the most successful Indian businessmen are from the Jain and the Vaishnav communities of Gujarat and Rajasthan. They are strict vegetarians. Since many foreign businessmen deal with them, they assume that all Indians are strict vegetarians as well. Jains are not Hindus (they do not worship Shiva, Vishnu or Brahma), though they fall in the larger framework of rebirth traditions (sanatan dharma). This Marwari and Bania culture also eclipses the vast non-vegetarian traditions of north India.

In the Puranas, Vishnu is a strictly vegetarian god, but Shiva eats whatever he is given and the Goddess loves blood. But we must remember that these are not strict rules. For when Vishnu descends as Ram, he hunts deer for food (an idea that many vegetarian Hindus reject rather violently). In Jain scriptures, Krishna is shown as participating in a wedding banquet of Neminath, where animals are slaughtered. Also as Narasimha, the man-lion avatar, Vishnu drinks blood. Shiva being a hermit accepts whatever he is offered. In his gentle Gora-Bhairav form, he is offered fruits and milk. In his fierce Kala-Bhairav form, he is offered blood and alcohol.

The Goddess is associated with nature's most elemental actions – sex and violence. She is offered blood. In the Varahi temples of Odisha, she eats fish. Yet, in many Goddess temples where she is closely associated with Vishnu, she is vegetarian, such as in the Amba-bai temple in Kolhapur, Maharashtra, or in the Goddess temples on the hills of Punjab and Jammu. So again, no fixed rule, even for the gods.

Some people equate vegetarianism with ahimsa or non-violence. Ahimsa is a fundamental principle of Jainism and yoga. However, ahimsa is a very complex idea. It means not hurting any living creature in body (tan) or mind (mann). But this does not extend to the act of eating. For all, the quest for food involves violence. Farming is a very violent activity involving the killing of many animals, not least the pests.

Many soldiers are vegetarian. Many corrupt politicians and crony capitalists who destroy the ecosystem with their industries or exploit workers in their factories are vegetarian. That is hardly non-violence! Many hermits give up meat to become spiritually pure. They have linked meat and blood to contamination. This is a dangerous idea: it forms the basis of 'untouchability' that renders certain people 'unclean' based on their traditional vocation which brings them in contact with flesh and blood. Turning 'blood' into contamination is the reason why women are seen as 'unclean' during periods and at the time of delivery. This disdain for blood as part of ritual purity fuels prejudice of the worst kind. Many vegetarian hermits think they are superior to meat-eating householders. This competition reveals the delusion created by the ego. We must be wary of this. We must keep reminding ourselves how the Goddess Kali demands blood sacrifice. Does it make the Goddess impure? Nature cannot be made impure and all of nature is the Goddess.

One must remember that when one denies Hindu pluralism one seeks to reframe Hinduism using Abrahamic templates.

Many Hindu supremacists do so to create a checklist of Hindu behaviours. They assume the practice of some dominant Brahmin and trading (Bania) communities as universal. One such practice happens to ally itself with food consumption: wherein they see 'non-vegetarian' as inferior and 'vegetarian' as more evolved, a belief that is less scientific and more designed to massage the ego. We must not forget that, in doing so, they deny the meat-eating practices of various nondominant communities. We must not forget that as per the food census, 70 per cent of India eats meat in some form or the other. We must not forget that Hinduism is not what some Brahmins and Banias decide it is, or should be. Brahminism is but a tiny subset of Hinduism, and not all Brahmins are vegetarian.

26

Is Holi celebrated everywhere in India?

Holi is generally celebrated in north India, not south India. No one knows the reason why. Of course, with north Indians migrating to south India for work, and as a result of the popularity of Bollywood, many regional festivals are becoming national. Holi is even celebrated in the Caribbean Islands by the Hindu descendants of indentured labour. It is celebrated by the diaspora, leading to the very popular, secular 'colour party' in many American universities.

Celebrated on the full moon day of spring, in the month of Phalgun (Feb-March), like most Hindu festivals, Holi has many layers. There is the Shaivite layer, the Vaishnava layer, and finally the Krishna layer. The festival has two parts, the bonfire on the night before and the wild colour celebration on the day after.

Attention to the Shaivite layer is drawn by the fact that the festival takes place a fortnight after Shivaratri and is also associated with the consumption of the intoxicating bhang (cannabis drink). The bonfire is associated with the burning of Kama-deva, the god of love, who tried to arouse Shiva's senses and was at the receiving end of the fiery glance of Shiva's third eye. The next day, however, on the appeal of Kama's wife, Rati, he was reborn, but without a body, and was hence renamed Ananga. His rebirth is celebrated with colour. Water is poured to douse the passions he arouses.

The Vaishnavaite layer speaks of how Vishnu destroyed those who tortured his devotee Prahalada. Holika who had the power to withstand fire hugged him and jumped into fire but ended up burning herself while Prahalada escaped unhurt thanks to the grace of Vishnu. The bonfire celebration marks the death of the wicked Holika.

The Krishna layer comes from the Gangetic plain and speaks of how Krishna celebrated this festival with Radha and the gopikas in Vrindavan. They mixed the flowers and leaves of the forest to create coloured water and poured it on each other. Celebrated with earthy lyrics, the festival does have a strong rural flavour, and lacks the sophistication and impersonality associated with urban spaces. It brings out the child in everyone and captures the spirit of Krishna's love for Radha. This festival captured the imagination of the Mughal kings who patronized it from the sixteenth century onwards. It was probably introduced by their Rajput queens.

Before long, Holi became part of the royal households

of north India – across Rajasthan and the hill states, while the temples of Krishna celebrated it in Gangetic plains, in Bihar, Assam, Bengal and Odisha. In the Jagannath temple, it became the Dola Poornima, when Krishna and Radha sit on swings and enjoy the spring. It is said that when Kama died, he was reborn as Krishna, and hence Holi marks the transformation of lust (kama) into love (prema).

These practices did not make it to the temple towns of south India where divinity was revered and adored but never quite seen in such familiar terms. Shiva was Dakshinamurti, the teacher of the Vedas and the Tantras. His antics as Bholenath, the guileless one, are more popular in the north than the south. Vishnu is the regal Ram and reclining Narayana. As Krishna he is more popular as a child. The adult Krishna is approached more through parental love (vatsalya bhakti), and the anguish of separation (viraha bhakti) than the tenderness of romance (madhurya bhakti). This could explain why, despite Krishna's popularity, Holi did not become very popular in the south.

This disparity reminds us of Hinduism's diversity and how its customs and beliefs are distributed differently in different parts of India and the world. Despite its popularity then, Holi is not quite a pan-Indian festival. It remains a primarily a north Indian festival, Bollywood songs notwithstanding.

27

Is there such a thing as
a Hindu Halloween?

Halloween, also known as Allhalloween, All Hallows' Eve, is a celebration popular in several western countries, predominantly America. People dress up as supernatural creatures, on the night of 31 October to drive away the ghosts who visit earth. It is traced to an old Celtic festival, Samhain, that saw this day, at the cusp of autumn and winter, as the day when the boundaries between the land of the dead and the land of the living become the thinnest. It falls a day before All Saint's Day (1 November). The following day is All Souls Day (2 November), when Christians pray to those who are in Heaven already and for the souls of the dead who wait for the Second Coming of Christ and the Day of Judgement.

But this concept is not limited to Abrahamic belief alone. All cultures have days when the dead are worshipped. This is closely linked to ghosts, who are believed to be restless souls who refuse to go to the land of the dead, and continue to linger in the land of the living, disturbing the cosmic balance, troubling the living to gain attention. In Hinduism, there is no exact equivalent of Halloween, but there are many rituals performed that recognize the proximity of ghosts and seek to force them or enable them to make the journey to the land of the dead, where they belong.

Every year, Pitr Paksha, the fortnight between the worship of Ganesha (Ganesha Chaturdashi) and the worship of Durga (Navaratri), is reserved for the ancestors (pitrs) of Hindus. This is when sarva-pitri-shraadh is done, to appease all the dead, who hang upside down, like bats, in Yama-loka, awaiting rebirth. During the ceremonies the living promise the dead that they will produce children to ensure their rebirth. However, the offering does not satisfy some pitrs and they turn into pretas, or ghosts.

There are different kinds of ghosts: bhoot, preta, pisacha and vetal. Those who lived incomplete lives do not want to go to the land of the dead and so stay back in the land of the living. Those who lived complete lives, but whose funeral rites were not performed properly, remain trapped in the land of the living. Some are cursed for their misdeeds, never to find peace in death and so haunt the living in misery. These are the ideas about ghosts that one gathers from various folklore and from the Garuda Purana, an elaborate treatise on death rituals.

In the Vedas, especially in the Atharva Veda, there are many hymns addressed to gods such as Indra, Agni and Soma, who are invoked to destroy fearful demons who emerge out of darkness. This indicates an awareness of malevolent spirits, and ghosts.

The Bhagavata Purana informs us that Brahma, in a state of laziness, created bhuta–pisachas or ghosts. They were naked and their hair was unbound. Seeing them he shut his eyes (in fear?).

> srṣṭvā bhūta-piśācāṁś ca
> bhagavān ātma-tandriṇā
> dig-vāsaso mukta-keśān
> vīkṣya cāmīlayad dṛśau
> – from Srimad-Bhagavat 3.20.40

Many gods and goddesses are linked to ghosts. They are invoked to drive ghosts away. The most popular of these is the gaunt Chamunda, who lives in crematoriums, is garlanded with the heads and limbs of men, and travels on the back of ghosts (preta). She is closely related to the wild Kotravai of the crematorium found in ancient Tamil lore.

The ghosts are also invoked by sorcerers who wished to control the pretas and turn them into powerful slaves. The most famous such story is that of Vikramaditya and the Vetala. In Odisha, where Tantra was widely practiced during medival times, there is a Vetal Deul in the capital city of Bhubaneshwar, associated with ghosts and exorcism.

In Kerala, there are tales of yakshis who seduce young men and gandharvas who seduce young women and either kill them or drive them mad. Those afflicted visit the temple of the goddess Chottanikkara Bhagavathy to be free of the ghosts. In this temple, ghosts are exorcized and driven away to the land of the dead. Similar rituals are performed in the Balaji Hanuman temple at Mehndipur, Rajasthan, where there is also a shrine dedicated to Pret-raj, the king of ghosts, a form of Yama. Another deity invoked to banish ghosts is Kal Bhairav Kotwal of Varanasi.

Basically, Hindus see ghosts as embodiments of malicious and adverse energies – the jealousy and hatred of others (living or dead) that can make them vulnerable to ailments and bad luck. The practice of hanging slippers on one's gateway is meant to frighten away ghosts. According to many folk rituals, lemons, chillies and rock salt are used to feed ghosts and keep them at bay while coal and iron are used to frighten them away.

Belief in ghosts acknowledges that we are surrounded by many unseen forces, positive and negative. These hidden forces were spirits and ghosts and, originally, spirituality meant faith in these unseen forces. Over time, spirituality has come to mean faith in god or the soul or energy – that force whose understanding still eludes scientists.

Faith: 40 Insights into Hinduism

28

Do Hindus lose their caste when they travel abroad?

If you value caste, then this thought can be depressing, even terrifying. If you are indifferent, it will not matter. In pre-modern times, caste was important, as it identified you as part of a community. This community gave one a profession and a spouse, and necessitated the following of the community diktats, which included giving one's daughter in marriage only to a member of the appropriate caste. One's caste, thus, functioned as an extended family. So, anything, that led to loss of caste acquired great consequence.

Baudhayana dharma-sutra, composed about 2000 years ago, maybe earlier, lists this 'Samudrolanghana' or 'Sagarollanghana' as first of many reasons for loss of castes (II.1.2.2). This especially applied to Brahmins, as there was fear that travel abroad prevented a Brahmin from performing various rites and rituals in the prescribed manner at the prescribed time. The belief was that movement away from the sacred Vedic fire made one vulnerable to pollution. The contemporary ritual of 'aarti' or waving of lamps when one is leaving the house is meant to create a shield to protect against pollution; the same ritual at the time of one's return is meant to wipe out all pollutants, and ensure purification.

The irony is that India has a long history of sea travel. Though the major epics, the Ramayana and the Mahabharata, do not refer to sea travel (Ram builds a bridge to go to Lanka, and Ravana flies in his Pushpak Viman), the vrata-kathas of India, like Satyanarayana Puja and the Topoye story of Odisha, and Sanskrit plays like *Ratnavali* by Harsha, refer to sea travel and shipwrecks. We do know that sea merchants travelled from India to Arabia in the West, in the Harappan era, 5000 years ago. There are Vedic verses that suggest (but not conclusively) people's awareness of the sea and sea travel nearly 3000 years ago. There was definitely a thriving sea trade with South East Asia in the Gupta period 1500 years ago. Sages like Agastya and Kaundinya did travel to faraway lands like Malaysia and Cambodia. The Chola kings travelled over the sea to Sri Lanka and Malaysia to expand their empire and to increase the wealth of the land through trade routes. Even today, in Odisha, and on the island of Bali, festivals celebrate the departure and arrival of ships, reminding us of ancient travel over sea. It is this sea travel that ensured that epics such as the Ramayana and the Mahabharata, the art of shadow puppetry and weaving, reached as far as Indonesia and Thailand.

Faith: 40 Insights into Hinduism

However, in medieval times, roughly 1000 years ago, after the age of Adi Shankaracharya, the arrival of Muslims and the collapse of Buddhism, we find the rise of an orthodox form of Hinduism that forbade sea travel. Sea trade continued but was outsourced to Arabs. The caste system become increasingly rigid and pollution a constant fear. No one knows what caused this shift.

Many theories have been proposed but none can be proved: maybe this was a kneejerk reaction to the violence of the new warlords who came from Central Asia and were breaking temples; maybe it was a way to destroy the merchant class who valued Buddhism and Jainism but not Brahmins; maybe it was to protect Hinduism from being diluted. At one time, this rule was fairly widespread and so strict that some communities even forbade their members from crossing certain rivers (some scholars argue that in Vedic Sanskrit 'samudra' means a large body of water, not necessarily the sea).

Some argue that in medieval times, while 'upper' castes shunned sea travel and outsourced it to Arabs, the 'lower' castes did continue to travel, and it was they who took Hinduism and Buddhism to South East Asia. While some Banias in north India refused to cross even the river Indus, others like the Chettiars of Tamil Nadu, did travel to Malaysia and Burma on ships, but they followed strict caste rules like celibacy and dietary restrictions, as well as the worship of the celibate Murugan and Shiva in both ports of call.

Although the Hindu Maratha rulers did establish a navy to combat Portuguese might, something neither the Muslim rulers nor the Deccan sultans did, it was about defending the borders of a newly established kingdom, not travelling and trading with another land.

When the Europeans finally wrested control of the sea trade from Arabs 500 years ago, a whole new way of thinking came to India. Suddenly the powerful rulers of India were not men who came on horseback such as the Mughals, but men who came in great ships such as the Portuguese, the French and the English. They wanted Indians to work on their ships. They recruited Indians into their armies, which fought on sea. After slavery was outlawed, they wanted indentured labour from India to work on their farms in faraway colonies in the Caribbean.

The fear of 'kalapani' or the black water of the sea that wipes out caste was at its peak in the nineteenth century. The East India Company faced a lot of problems with the Brahmins they recruited in their army, who refused to cross the sea. So, the worst punishment they came up with, after the 1857 Uprising, was to incarcerate them as political prisoners in the Cellular Jail on Andaman, across the Bay of Bengal, infamous as the Kala-Pani Jail, for going there meant loss of caste and social excommunication for Brahmin revolutionaries.

Hindus who travelled abroad in the nineteenth century faced a lot of problems. Raja Ram Mohan Roy, for example. Swami Vivekananda too was criticized, but he took it in his characteristic stride as he spread the ideas of Hinduism in America. In the film, *Man Who Knew Infinity*, based on the mathematician, Ramanujan, we find references to this rule. But as education in England came to be valued, as China became the land for the lucrative opium trade, and job opportunities opened in America, economic and political reality meant that old Brahmin diktats had to change.

In the last 100 years, people have, to a large extent, become relaxed about it. It still matters in certain circles, like for the high priests of Tirupati temple, the seers of Udupi Krishna temple and in some Kerala temples, for example, and even leads to court battles. But like all things Hindu, there always is a way through. There are cleansing rites (shuddhi): the chanting of certain mantras and fasting, suggested for those who return home. This is satisfactory for most traditional Brahmin families. Most, not all.

29

Why is conversion not a practice in Hinduism?

Hinduism is not founded on the concept of 'false' gods and 'true' gods. It has no philosophy of any god acting as a 'judge'. Here, the idea of truth is seen very differently: there is limited truth or mithya, and limitless truth or satya. The finite human mind can never appreciate the infinity of the world. But the mind can be expanded – by practices such as yoga and tapasya and tantra propagated by hermits.

Only the sage can see all. He is therefore Buddha, he whose intelligence (buddhi) is fully formed. He is therefore bhagavan, he who sees all parts (bhaga). In Jainism and Buddhism, the sage is a great teacher. In Hinduism, the sage is god, who defies the mortal body. The God of Hinduism is limitless (ananta). This limitless god can 'contract' himself and 'bring himself down to the level of mortals'. From here comes the concept of 'avatar' (he who descends). From his mountaintop, Shiva sees all. But he lives there in isolation. So, the Goddess brings him down to the plains, to Kashi, where the gaze is restricted by the horizon.

God who is 'limitless' is very different from god who rejects the 'false'. The one is accommodating of all human limitation. The other cannot accept human weakness. The one has no sense of urgency for he sees fear of death as delusion. The other wants to save the world before falsehood claims the world. The one is at peace. The other is always at war.

Guess which god dominates the modern world?

Ironically, the Hindu Right wing have started adopting the Abrahamic version of God. And the Left wing, too, seems to agree with this definition of god. It has become the only definition of god, endorsed even by atheists and Bollywood.

The limitless god is too passive – he does not indulge cult leaders. Cult leaders want to be admired as heroes, and so they need villains. They construct 'false gods' – missionaries and secularists. They reject post-modern definitions of mythology. For them myth is 'falsehood' not 'subjective truth'. The latter definition does not serve their ambitions. There is an epidemic of cult leaders in the Right wing, desperately seeking power, each one a jealous god. They don't care for any truth but their own. They tell stories of how Hinduism is under threat and how everyone needs to be alert and fight back. But there is one key clause in a cult leader's story that often goes unnoticed: to win the battle against Christian missionaries, you must recognize only their version of Hinduism, with them being its true articulators. Thus, they make themselves the chosen one! Other than cult followers, everyone can see the irony.

We often forget that one of the earliest forms of 'conversion' can be traced to Buddhism. It did this without force, without violence – through one leader (Buddha), one clear doctrine and set of rules (Dhamma), and institutions (the sangha). Buddhist monks did not speak of any 'true' or 'false' gods, but they did offer the 'cure for worldly suffering' revealed by their leader. For the common folk, this made Buddha the source of the solution, a larger-than-life being, greater than man – a god! So eventually, ignoring earlier practices, gigantic images of Buddha started appearing, and being worshipped, in Central Asia, China and South East Asia. He who did not care for the gods, became a god. And when he became god, the many Gods of the Puranas, from Shiva to Kali to Krishna, ended up overshadowing him.

Many believe that Jesus was greatly influenced by Buddhism in his 'lost years' and was inspired to create the 'church', an idea that was alien to the earlier Jewish faith. When the church became powerful, the Roman empire adopted it. Instead of conquering tax-paying land for Rome, the new generals began conquering souls for the one true God. Later, with the rise of science, god became secular 'money', and the age of enlightenment became the age of colonization. Secular thought propagated itself on the principles of the church – lessons of conversion informed many a marketing department. Brands and rockstars are now the new gods.

Conversion believes that only one story will prevail in the end. Re-conversion believes that some stories are under threat. The tangible form of stories – customs, rituals, symbols – may die. The language (vac, in the Vedas) may die but not the thought (manas, in the Vedas). The intangible form of every story is eternal (sanatan, in the Vedas) and ever-changing (a-nitya, in the Vedas).

We forget that stories influence stories. Just as Buddhism can influence Christianity, and Christianity can influence Capitalism and Communism, and the story of the 'one true God' can influence truth-seeking scientists, similarly, the story of the 'limitless god' of Hinduism can also influence the limited truths of terrorists and activists.

Hinduism does not believe in changing people's minds or replacing old ideas. It believes in expanding their minds and adding new ideas. Hence, there is no need to convert, just enlighten empathize and accommodate.

Scriptures

30

What are the Vedas?

Hinduism's roots lie in what are called the Vedas. People are divided on whether this refers to a set of texts, or simply to the idea of atma. The latter is differentiated from the former by being called Vedanta.

Over 3000 years ago, chants known as mantras were used during ritual yagnas that played a key role in society. Manuals that explained how these rituals ought to be conducted were known as the brahmanas, so called because the rituals helped invoke the Brahman, or the great mysterious force that animates the cosmos. Compiled, these mantras came to be known as samhitas or collections. The earliest of these collections was the Rig Samhita. The wisdom they contained was known as veda or knowledge. Later other collections came into being, such as Yajur and Sama and Atharva, containing in varying numbers the hymns of the Rig Samhita. The keepers of these manuals and performers of these rituals came to be known as Brahmins. The ritualistic approach was known as karma kanda. Later, this path would come to be known as purva mimansa, meaning early investigations.

Many people saw the mantras very differently. They felt that the hymns had to be heard and contemplated upon. Contemplation would reveal metaphysical truths about the cosmos. This intellectual approach was known as gyan kanda, and eventually it came to be known as uttara mimansa, meaning later investigations. This approach led to the compilation of texts known as aranyaka or forest-texts, indicating that those who celebrated this approach were hermits, very different in character from Brahmins who lived and thrived within society. Many believe that the forest-texts were written by kings and warriors who rejected the ritualistic Brahmins. These aranyakas were compiled and are now known as the Upanishads – dialogues and discussions on the nature of reality. King Janaka is believed to have called a great conference where these ideas were discussed. The discussion was so profound that it was concluded that it marked the peak of Vedic wisdom or Vedanta. It is here that we find ideas such as atma, or the true self, that forms the cornerstone of Hindu thought.

Who were the rishis then? They were the poet-sages closely associated with Vedic wisdom. Were they the city-dwellers or forest-dwellers? This is not clear. In mythology, they are performers of both yagna as well as tapasya. Yagna was an external ritual while tapasya was a spiritual practice that involved withdrawing from the material world and engaging in contemplation, concentration and meditation.

Some people classify the forest-dwellers further. There were the alchemists or tantriks and the analysts or yogis. Tantriks appreciated the material world as power or shakti, that could – through various practices – be manipulated at will. Yogis saw the material world as a delusion or maya. Through analysis (samkhya) and synthesis (yoga) of hymns as well as experience, they could look beyond the material world and experience spiritual reality.

As time passed, society found it difficult to relate to the ritualistic Brahmins or the forest-dwelling hermits, with their esoteric practices and highbrow philosophy. They turned to the simple ways propagated by the monk-teachers or shramanas. They brought the wisdom of the forest-ascetics to the masses. While the Brahmins said that all problems could be solved through ritual, the shramanas said that all problems were creations of the mind. The method of solving them was austerity and meditation. The path of austerity was propagated by the monk-teachers of the Jain faith. The path of meditation was propagated by the monk-teachers of the Buddhist faith. This happened around 500 BCE.

Brahmins soon realized that they were losing ground to Buddhism and Jainism. They had to redefine themselves and reach out to the common man. Vedic truths could not remain in an elitist framework restricted to priests and philosophers. They had to reach the masses. And the method for this was stories.

Stories have always been a part of ritual tradition. Stories were told to entertain priests and kings who performed yagnas. Gradually stories became the vehicle of Vedic truths, so much so that the act of listening to the story was equated to performing the yagna. In stories, the most profound Vedic thought was captured symbolically and narratively. The religion that spread through stories is often differentiated from the religion that existed prior to the arrival of the shramanas. The pre-Buddhist religion is called Vedism to distinguish it from the post-Buddhist religion now known as Hinduism.

Hinduism spread through stories. And stories propagated three ideas: karma yoga, bhakti yoga and gyan yoga. Karma yoga or the path of action was different from the earlier karma kanda. Earlier, action was all about conducting rituals; but later, action became all about performing social duties and obligations. Stories basically celebrated the householder's life over the hermit's. Bhakti yoga or the path of devotion gave form to the ancient Vedic notion of brahman, the impersonal divine force invoked during the yagna. This gave rise to the idea of God. Through stories, people were encouraged to have an emotional relationship with God. Gyan yoga or the path of introspection gave an intellectual foundation to karma yoga and bhakti yoga. It was propagated by teachers or acharyas such as Shankara, Abhinavagupta, Ramanuja, Madhava and Vallabha. This was essentially Vedic wisdom, or what is now called Vedanta.

The Brahmins realized that ritual played an important role in binding communities. So, rituals were not completely forsaken.

They fused rituals into stories. Newer rituals emerged, simpler rituals, that took the place of the earlier yagna. Some of the stories invariably revolved around an image or a holy site. So, began the practice of visiting holy places, taking dips in holy rivers and pools and most importantly going and looking at sacred images housed in temples. This became the act of darshan or looking at a sacred image and it was, like the act of listening to a story, equated with getting in touch with Vedic truths. One of the rituals that replaced yagna was puja, which evoked divinity in an otherwise lifeless object. People now began making offerings to images, recognizable anthropomorphic images, and not just fire. Eventually, grand temple complexes were built around rocks, stone and metal images that were transformed into sources of divine energy.

Puja could also augment the personal relationship of man and the divine. And so apart from the temples outside the house, people were encouraged to create temples inside the house. God became a living entity who could simultaneously be housed in the village temple and the household temple. He was treated as an august guest, showered with food, clothing and gifts. Unlike Vedic gods who were distant, reachable only through yagna, the later Hindu gods became accessible and tangible.

This transformation, from the ritual, through the intellectual, to the emotional, has ensured the survival of Vedic truths in India for over 3000 years. There was a time when there was a wide gap between the ritual-texts and the forest-texts. A similar gap is emerging today. On one side are the stories, the rituals and the fantastic images of Hinduism. On the other side are the philosophies gleaned from Vedic texts. Not many are able to see the link between the two. Understanding this yoke is the need of the hour.

31

What is the Tamil Veda?

 One finds three books identified as the Tamil Veda (known locally as Dravida Veda or Tamil Marai):

- Tirukkural, a secular book of 1330 ethical sayings, by Valluvar, which is over 2000 years old and of probable Jain origin.

- Tevaram, a Shaiva book of nearly 800 devotional songs, by Nayanars, which is also over 1000 years old. The songs are sung in the Shaiva shrines of south India, and given preference over Sanskrit Vedic hymns.

- Divya Prabhandham, a Vaishnava book of 4000 devotional songs, by Alvars, which is over 1000 years old. These songs are sung in the Vaishanva shrines of south India, and given preference over Sanskrit Vedic hymns.

e composed in the Indus plains about 4000

re organized in the Rig Veda and attached to

ar Veda and to melodies in the Sama Veda in

ains about 3000 years ago. Around 2500 years

t (shramana) traditions such as Buddhism and

Jain... nged the ritualism of the householder traditions, and declared their preference for Prakrit over Sanskrit. These hermits travelled south along with Vedic Brahmins.

Some theorize that these are the rishis that Ram encountered as he moved south towards Godavari; they told him about the vanaras (monkey tribes) of Kishkinda, the modern Deccan plateau, and the rakshasas (demon tribes) who lived further south. But this is speculation.

The first epigraphic evidence of civilizations in the Indian subcontinent comes from the Ashokan edicts, 2300 years ago, and the Kharavela inscriptions, 2100 years ago, that refer for the first time to the southern kingdoms of the Cholas, Pandyas and Cheras. Archaeologists have found the Tamil Brahmi script, and even cities, dated to this period in Tamil Nadu, and Roman gold coins in ports, indicating a thriving sea trade. Here was spoken old Tamil, which eventually gave rise to other languages such as Telugu, Kannada, Tulu and Malayalam.

Over 2000 years ago, roughly when the Ramayana and the Mahabharata and even the dharma-shastras were being composed in north India, Tamil lands saw the composition of poems about love and longing (the inner or akam poetry) and about war (the outer or puram poetry). Many years after it was written, this body of literature came to be known as Sangam (assembly) poetry. They reveal a familiarity with Vedic rituals as well as with Buddhism and Jainism, indicating that northern ideas have moved south 2000 years ago.

About 1500 years ago, Tamil poets were composing great epics such as Shillapadikaram and Manimeghalai in which women and hermits play a central role. They reveal the popularity of Jainism and Buddhism in the region that is today Tamil Nadu, Andhra Pradesh, Kerala and Karnataka. These clearly overshadowed local Vedic Brahmins, which in turn led to much rivalry.

The Veda-carrying Brahmins had come to the south in waves. We know the earliest version of the Sanskrit Mahabharata, written using Sharada script, reached Kerala via Brahmins who wore their topknots in front (purva-shikha). Later, Brahmins who wore their top knot behind (apara-shikha) carried another version of the Sanskrit Mahabharata which became the more voluminous manuscript in Grantha script. These Hindu epics came with ideas about Shiva and Vishnu that started mingling with Dravidian deities such as Murugan, the warlord who stands atop mountains, and Kotravai, the goddess of battle.

Then around 1200 years ago came a man from Kerala called Adi Shankara, who travelled north via Omkara to Kashi, and then toured all over India doing something remarkable: he resurrected Vedic thinking by reframing it differently using Puranic gods. He connected the old Vedic traditions (Nigama) to the later Puranic traditions (Agama) associated with pilgrimage, and worship of icons in temples. He challenged the intellectual traditions of the Buddhists and established the hermit-seer (acharya) tradition within Hinduism. He inspired many scholars to write Sanskrit commentaries on the nature of God based on the Upanishads and the Bhagavad Gita.

Around the same time, Brahmins like Nathamuni compiled the hymns of Alvar poets, and even composed a few. Later, acharyas like Ramanuja, renowned for his scholarship as well as administrative skills, who lived a 1000 years ago, integrated the Vaishnava Tamil Veda (Diyva Prabandham) with temple rituals in Shrirangam and other major Vaishnava temple complexes. Likewise, Nayanar poet-saints such as Sambandhar and Appar composed songs in praise of Shiva, challenging the ways of the Jains, the Buddhists and even the Vaishnavas. The Shaiva Tamil Veda (Tevaram) was integrated with Shiva Siddhanta philosophy and temple rituals in Chidambaram and other Shaiva temple complexes. They found royal patronage from the Pallava, Chola and Pandya kings.

In Tamil imagination, everything started much earlier. At the dawn of time, Shiva gave a discourse on the Vedas and so all sages moved north; this caused the earth to tilt and so Shiva ordered his best student, Agastya, to move south. Agastya came carrying northern mountains such as Palni on his shoulders and northern rivers such as Kaveri in his pot. He even organized Tamil grammar. He passed his knowledge on to his students, one of whom wrote the Tolkappiyam, the earliest available work on Tamil grammar.

About 1200 years ago, around the time of Adi Shankara, a commentary on Tolkappiyam informs us about three grand assemblies of poet-saints organized by Pandyan kings and attended by gods, where Tamil poetry was presented. Tsunami-like floods washed away the coastal cities where the first two assemblies took place. Recent archaeological digs suggest that the third assembly may have taken place in ancient Madurai, maybe 2000 years ago.

All this talk of grand Tamil cities, with assemblies of poet-sages, with trading links to South East Asia and to the Middle East, that washed away in the floods, has led to the theory that the Dravidian language thrived in the Harappan civilization, 5000 years ago, before being displaced by Sanskrit-speaking Aryans. This thesis of Tamil being pushed away from the north is popular among many south Indians. By contrast, many north Indians believe that from the beginning of time, or at least 12000 years ago, across the Indian subcontinent, even in cities of Harappan civilization, Sanskrit, the language of the gods, was spoken, and Tamil is just a branch of Sanskrit. Neither of these are scholarly claims; they are political and best left to politicians.

What we can be certain of is that Tamil literature has a history of over 2000 years. It gave us a secular Tamil Veda, Tirukurral, as it exchanged ideas with Vedic, Buddhist and Jain cultures. About 1000 years ago, the literature gave us the Shaiva and Vaishnava Tamil Vedas of the Nayanar and Alvar poet-saints that erupted into the bhakti way of thinking that transformed Hinduism forever.

This period of intense connection with God marks a revolution in Hinduism: at one level, the yagna rituals were completely sidelined by temple rituals, and at another level people were giving more importance to emotional relationships with God, over ritual connections via priests. It witnessed Kamban retelling the Ramayana in Tamil, which in turn inspired other poets to retell the Ramayana in their local tongues. Thus, we find multiple Ramayanas gradually appearing in the south, in the east and finally in the north and the west. Scholars are now convinced that the origin of passionate bhakti and a private relationship between devotee and deity, bypassing temples and Brahmins, originated in the south and spread to the north. We can say that the Tamil Veda marks the rise of the bhakti movement of India about a 1000 years ago.

32

What exactly is the Manusmriti?

The Manusmriti presents itself as a document that compiles and organizes code of conduct for human society. It came into being roughly 1800 years ago, around the same time that yagna-based Vedic Hinduism transformed into temple-based Puranic Hinduism. It stands for 'code of Manu' but literally it means 'reflections of Manu'. Therefore, people assume that the Manusmriti is the law book of Hindus, something like the sharia of Muslims, or Church dogma of Catholic Christians, or the Constitution of India. But this assumption is incorrect. It is a code of conduct put together by Brahmins, mainly for Brahmins, and maybe for other 'upper' caste communities, especially the king. It is part of a set of documents known as dharma-shastras.

The Manusmriti was composed roughly around 200 CE. We know this because it refers to Saka (north-west tribes)

and Cheen (China) who established contact with India around this time. It also refers to gold coins which, as per archaeological evidence, started being used around this time. And it is referred to in books composed around this time, like the Kama Sutra.

The Manusmriti is unique among the dharma-shastras as it presents itself like a holy text, a Purana, beginning with the origin of the world, the origin of the four communities (varna), the law for the four communities, managing situation in time of adversities, rectifying situation that follows transgression, and finally the two great conclusions of human life, either obtaining the fruits of this life's actions in the next life, or liberating oneself from the cycle of birth and death.

Unlike the Vedas, which are called shruti, that which is heard, and considered eternal divine revelations, the Manusmriti or Manava-dharma-shastra, is a smriti (that which is recollected), the work of man, subject to change with time (kala), place (sthana) and participants (patra).

Hindus believe that to make life meaningful (purusha-artha), we have to pursue four goals simultaneously: be socially responsible (dharma), generate and distribute wealth (artha), indulge in pleasure (kama) and not get too attached to anything (moksha). Knowledge related to each of these four pursuits when organized is called shastra. Thus, we have dharma-shastra, artha-shastra, kama-shastra and moksha-shastra.

These shastras started being compiled by Brahmins roughly from the time of the Mauryan emperors. Initially they were composed as prose and to aid memorization, sentences were short and terse. These were the sutras. Later, prose gave way to poetry (shloka).

Apasthambha, Gautama, Baudhayana compiled the earliest dharma-shastras; Chanakya compiled the artha-shastra; Vatsyayana compiled the kama-shastra; and various philosophers such as Patanjali and Badarayana compiled different kinds of moksha-shastra, such as yoga and Vedanta. Note the use of the word 'compiled', as these scholars always acknowledged that they were part of a larger and older tradition, and their knowledge had originated outside them, in the Vedas.

The origin of the Manusmriti is attributed to Brahma, the creator, who passes it on to the first human, Manu, who passes it on to the first teacher, Bhrigu, who passes it on to other sages. Since its composition, it has been seen as the foremost dharma-shastra, overshadowing all other law books. Maximum commentaries on dharma-shastras use the Manusmriti as the code book. The content can be traced back to the Vedas, and to the custom and practices of those who know the Veda.

The Manusmriti aligns with the Vedic view that society is composed of four kinds of communities: those who know the Vedas (Brahmins), those who govern the land (Kshatriyas), those who trade (Vaishyas) and those who serve (Shudra). Typically, dharma-shastras give greater value to the code of Brahmins than to that of Kshatriyas. Statecraft is elaborated in the artha-shastra. However, the Manusmriti gives almost equal value to the code of Brahmins and that of Kshatriyas, effectively making the artha-shastra a part of the dharma-shastra. So, while earlier dharma-shastras were interested in regulating the conduct of Brahmins mainly, the Manusmriti is also interested in regulating the conduct of Kshatriyas as well.

Of the nearly 2500 verses, over 1000 are meant for Brahmins, over 1000 for the king, only 8 for Vaishyas and 2 for Shudras. Clearly, the focus is not all of society, but only Brahmins, and their relationship with kings. This strategy ensured that Brahmins had success and significance, despite the rise of Buddhism and Jainism. This trend prevailed over time, even during the Mughal era, right down to the Brahmin domination of the bureaucracy in British times and even post-Independence.

In the nineteenth century, many Europeans celebrated the Manusmriti for affirming life, and they saw Manu in opposition to the world-denying monastic Buddha, who was also becoming popular around that time in Europe as a noble sage. Recommended reading in the nineteenth century for the educated included passages from the Manusmriti. In the twentieth century, things changed. As caste became an important political issue, Manu was seen as institutionalizing the caste system, and Buddha rejecting it. The Manusmriti was then seen as the source of India's inequalities which led to many acts of public burning of the books.

The Manusmriti was one of the many dharma-shastras, and it was not much in use as India came to be increasingly governed by Muslim rulers, such as the sultans of Delhi and Deccan and Bengal. When the British East India Company took over the governance of India from the Mughals, they compiled laws for managing their subjects. For Muslims, they accepted the then prevalent sharia law, but for Hindus, they had nothing. So, they resurrected the Manusmriti and treated it as a Hindu law book, which was never its intention. This made the Manusmriti famous throughout the world. Until this time, the status of women and castes in Indian society was rather fluid, varying as per regional contexts. But the British fixed it. This eventually paved the way for the 'divide and rule' policy of the British, and the 'vote bank' politics after Independence.

The Manusmriti was written at a time when, according to genetic science, caste groups were becoming progressively endogamous with strict rules against inter-caste marriage (even today less than 10 per cent of marriages in India are inter-caste). This means that caste as an institution, prohibiting inter-caste marriage, became rather inflexible – roughly 2000 years ago. But this did not happen *because* of the Manusmriti. The Manusmriti was never culpable of what it stands accused of. It was merely a documentation of already prevalent social practices. It was never meant to be taken as creed for *all* Hindus, but as a code primarily for Brahmins. It would probably have been disremembered, lost in libraries, meant for specialist scholars only, had the British not used it as an instrument to help them rule their colony.

33

Does the Law of Manu sanction the caste system?

Hindus never had law books like the Judaic Talmud or the Islamic Hadith or a guiding vision statement like the Declaration of Man produced in 1789 during the French Revolution. In this vein, one can say that the Manusmriti is *not* a Hindu law book.

From around the fifth century BCE, some Brahmins decided to write down how they thought society should behave. These books were known as the dharma-shastras. These were not pan-Hindu but localized to kingdoms where the Brahmins served. A key theme of this scripture was adaptability as per space, time and people (sthana, kala, patra).

In the nineteenth century, when the British were codifying laws for their Indian colonies, they decided to look for a book that would help them create laws for Hindus. They assumed that the laws would be with Brahmins. After all, were priests not the keepers of law in the Christian faith? The Brahmins of Benares gave them texts that most closely resembled what these colonial lawmakers were seeking – the dharma-shastras.

There are many dharma-shastras, one of which is the Manusmriti. Their influence in Indian society is anybody's supposition, considering Hinduism is not as dogmatic as Abrahamic religions tend to be. The British selected the Manusmriti simply on the assumption that Manu of the Manusmriti was the Hindu 'Adam'. This was all part of the colonial exercise to document and homogenize Hinduism for administrative convenience. Manusmriti means 'reflections of Manu'; the British made it 'laws of Manu'.

The Manusmriti and all other dharma-shastras mixed the concept of 'jati' with the concept of 'varna'. Jati is a social concept, and varna was initially a psychological concept. Jati referred to professional guilds that had existed in India since Buddhist times, around 500 BCE. The concept of varna came from Vedic scriptures. It was based on natural qualities (guna) and was more metaphorical than real.

The Vedas declared that every society is a man-made organism, whose head is made up of those who pursue knowledge (Brahmin), arms by those who pursue power (Kshatriya), torso of those who pursue wealth (Vaishya), and legs by those who provide service (Shudra). Manu mapped the hundreds of jatis to the four-fold varna framework. Those who did not fit any of the four varnas, were included in a fifth group (Panchama).

However, this neat four-fold structure is rather theoretical. In practice, there are the upper castes (savarna) and the lower castes (avarna, or Dalits), the former having access to political and economic power, and the latter having none. In fact, many members of the lower castes were considered ceremonially unclean. This idea of 'ritual pollution' is most evident in Hindu rituals, but is part of a larger South Asian cultural belief system.

Pakistan and Bangladesh are Muslim countries. Their residents converted to Islam centuries ago but they still follow caste hierarchies, especially when it comes to giving jobs related to sewage to 'low castes'. Sri Lanka, which has always been a Buddhist nation and had little or no Hindu influence also has a caste hierarchy, which cannot be explained using the 'law of Manu'.

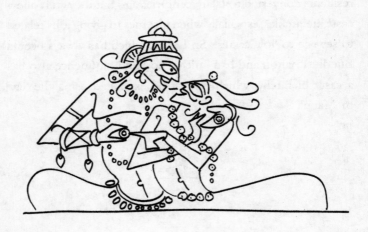

34

What do the Manusmriti and the dharma-shastras have to say about homosexuality?

Ⅰndia's Supreme Court decriminalised homosexuality in 2018, reading down a colonial law, which in turn was based on Abrahamic mythology. That anti-homosexual colonial law (still followed in erstwhile colonies of Asia and Africa) involved a reading – some would say, a deliberate misreading – of the tale where God destroys the cities of Sodom and Gomorrah with fire and brimstone because they perform acts that go against his commandment. What these acts were is open to all kinds of interpretation, again subject to how one interprets the old Aramaic, Hebrew and Greek scripts.

The anti-queer lobby claims that city dwellers indulged in homosexual behaviour. The queer supporters interpret the story differently, inferring that the city dwellers were not good hosts, and they raped their guests. Take your pick. What is curious is that soon after this incident, the patriarch, Lot, who runs out of Sodom and Gomorrah before they are destroyed, has sex with his own daughters, but this incestuous act is not punished by God.

Such tales, of God prohibiting certain sexual acts but allowing others, are not found in Hindu mythology. While in many Abrahamic traditions, homosexuality is seen as an act against God, in Hindu traditions, homosexuality is seen as part of karma. We are creatures of karma, and our actions contribute to our future karma. Thus, homosexuality is believed to be a manifestation of karma. We cannot fight it. We should deal with it.

Just as heterosexual desire needs to be regulated, so does homosexual desire. The extent of regulation varies depending on context. Some believe sex is only for producing children, some believe only people in love should have sex, while some believe sex is just a form of pleasure and must not be taken too seriously. The Vedas speak of Agni, the fire-god, having two mothers! Must this be taken literally or metaphorically?

In the Puranas, God changes gender constantly: Every god has a female Shakti: Vinayaka has Vinayaki, Varaha has Varahi. Shiva becomes Ardhanareshwara, or half-woman, to make the Goddess happy. He becomes Gopeshwar to join Krishna in the raas-leela. In the Baul tradition, when Kali decides to become Krishna, Shiva takes the form of Radha. Vishnu becomes the damsel Mohini to enchant demons and sages. In the Tulsi Ram-charit-manas, God says that he loves all creatures: plants, animals, men, women and queers (napunsaka), who give up malice and surrender to his grace. How does one read this? A comfort with gender and sexual fluidity? An acceptance of karma?

Medical texts, such as Shushruta Samhita, subscribe to the Tantrik belief that when a man and woman procreate, the gender and sexuality of the child depend on the proportion of the male white seed and female red seed. If the male white seed is stronger then heterosexual men are born; when the female red seed is stronger, then heterosexual females are born. When both seeds are equally strong, the child becomes queer (kliba, napunsaka, kinnara). Sanskrit texts on astrology, architecture and music refer to all three genders: male, female and queer. Thus, the condition is seen as physiological, not pathological.

The dharma-shastras need to be located in this context. They were books that speculated on appropriate human conduct. Written by Brahmins in the period that saw the composition of the Ramayana and the Mahabharata, they have a relatively casual attitude towards non-vaginal (ayoni) sex. This could even refer to anal/oral sex between consenting adult men and women, not just between men, or between women.

The Arthashastra of Kautilya charges a fine, similar to fines for minor thefts. Women are fined more than men. The fine increases if one of the partners is not consenting. (IV. XIII.236)

The Manusmriti equates homosexual sex to a man having sex with a menstruating woman, or having sex during the day, and the punishment involves purification rites: bathing with clothes on, fasting for a night, and then consuming the milk and urine of a cow. Failure to purify can result in loss of caste. The crimes of heterosexual adultery and rape, and deflowering a virgin, have far higher fines and more intense purification rituals. (XI:175)

The dharma-shastras clearly value heterosexual marriage and sex that results in the birth of sons. They acknowledged, grudgingly, the existence of other forms of sex and sought to curb them, without overtly condemning them, like all forms of sexual misconduct.

In monastic orders, like Buddhism and Jainism, where celibacy is celebrated, sexual desire, be it homosexual or heterosexual, is seen as obstacle to the spiritual path. In Charvaka, or materialistic traditions, the intrinsic nature (svabhava) of living creatures must be appreciated and admired, rather than judged. Thus, India has had a very varied, generally open-minded, stance towards all kinds of sex, including homosexuality, with warnings about compulsion, attachment and obsession.

History

35

Is Hinduism an Aryan religion?

What is the meaning of the word 'Aryan'? If by Aryan, one thinks of Nazism, then it is incorrect. If by Aryan one means a people who spoke the Proto-Indo-European (PIE) language, and who migrated into India from Eurasia via Central Asia about 4000 years ago, and composed Vedic lore over 1000 years, as they moved from the Indus to the Gangetic plains, then it would be correct – but only partly.

Until the advent of genetic studies, information on Aryans was restricted to linguistic studies of two ancient scriptures: the Avesta of Iran and the Vedas of India. Archaeological evidence was sparse. This led to lots of speculation, with fierce arguments on whether Aryans came into India or spread out of India. Which was their original homeland? Eurasia or India?

However, now genetic studies have clearly revealed that horses were domesticated in Eurasia 6000 years ago, and migrations out of Eurasia began 5000 years ago. One branch moved west towards Europe and another east towards Asia. Both these branches were familiar with horses and chariots with spoked wheels. The Asian branch distinguished itself by its knowledge of hoama/soma ritual. Eventually it split into the Iranian branch and the Indian branch, the former using the word 'deva' for demons, and tilting towards monotheism, and the latter using the word 'deva' for gods, and leaning towards polytheism.

The composers of the Veda reveal great familiarity with a river called Saraswati, now called Ghaggar. This indicates they were familiar with the cities we now know as the Harappan civilization, that spread over most of north-west India and were clustered around the river Indus and the now-drying Saraswati-Ghaggar. This culture was declining, or probably even dead, when the Aryans came into India. Scholars are not entirely sure. What is clear is that seals from the Indus valley bear images of elephants and tigers but not horses, and Vedic hymns are obsessed with horses and show unfamiliarity with elephants and tigers.

Research has shown that the cities of the Indus valley collapsed because of climate change, not invasion, long before Vedic hymns were compiled, or composed. Genetic data has revealed that genetic mixing was common in India 4000 years ago: meaning the 'Aryans' who composed the Rig Veda were already mingling with the descendants of the Harappan cities. They were neither invaded nor enslaved, as European orientalists imagined, but contributed to the hymns and lore.

Rigid marriage rules based on caste that created unique genetic clusters can be traced only from around 2000 years ago. So while the Vedas may speak of social stratification (varna), the hierarchical rigid vocation-based caste system (jati) emerged much later, over a thousand years later, and was not an Aryan invention. But this colonial propaganda still rings true owing to its simplicity.

In the nineteenth century, Aryan referred to some kind of a super-race of fair complexioned, blue-eyed, blonde warriors who came on war-chariots from Europe and invaded Iran and then smashed their way into India by overpowering the cities of the Indus valley and enslaving their people. This was political propaganda to justify European colonization. German nationalists used it to celebrate their pre-Semitic Nazi heritage. The British used it to delegitimize Hindus, claiming that 'upper caste' Hindus were as much invaders and conquerors of India, as Muslims and Europeans, and so had no moral right to claim India as homeland.

In the twenty-first century, many Hindu nationalists, or rather Hindu supremacists, are convinced that India is the original home of the Aryans. They communicated pure and perfect and complete Vedic knowledge before contamination by 'outsiders' like the Greeks and Muslims and Europeans. This is called the Out of India Theory. Anyone who does not agree with this theory is deemed anti-national and anti-Hindu, so the argument has become more political than academic. The Out of India theory emerged in the 1980s. According to this, India is the homeland of the Aryans. The Aryans composed the Vedas and built the Indus valley cities. They migrated to Iran, and thence to Europe. Although this argument is based on sound logic, recent genetic studies clearly tilt the evidence in favour of Aryan migration. Later research may prove otherwise.

The Aryans entered the Indian subcontinent around 4000 years ago, a period when the cities of the Indus-Saraswati valleys had already declined. The Aryans brought horses and PIE language with them, but not quite the Vedas. In the Indus valley, and dry riverbeds of Saraswati, in the decaying brick cities, as they mingled with local people who had memories of the great river Saraswati that once flowed in this region, they refined old hymns, composed new ones that were eventually compiled to form the Rig Veda, in a language we now know as Vedic, or pre-Panini, or pre-classical, Sanskrit. This language has nearly 300 words borrowed from the Munda language, considered as a pre-Vedic Indian language, indicating local influence. About 3000 years ago, the migration continued eastwards to the lush green Gangetic plains, where the Yajur, Sama and Atharva Vedas were composed. Here, eventually, 2500 years ago, the Upanishadic revolution and the rise of Buddhist and Jain monastic orders refined one idea that makes Indic thought unique: faith in karma, or rebirth.

We must be careful of the 'politics of origin' according to which a land belongs to the people who originated there; this delegitimizes all immigrants and nomads. We must be careful also of the 'politics of purity' that is hostile to all foreigners. Our earliest ancestors emerged from Africa, and populated the whole world, forming various groups, tribes, clans, races, ethnicities, communities and nationalities. Due to natural calamities (climate change, famine) and cultural calamities (war), people have had to migrate repeatedly in different directions, often returning to spaces their ancestors abandoned thousands of years earlier. Thus, every land is populated by waves of people who have come in at different points of time, from different spaces, each one bringing new ideas and new technologies. There is no such thing as a pure and homogenous society. Every society is hybrid and heterogeneous. This is perhaps the reason the Puranas say that even if we have different fathers, we have a common grandfather, Brahma. And it is okay, if he was African.

In conversations about Aryans, we need to ask ourselves: Why do we give race so much importance? Why is it important to prove that the Indus valley and the Vedas are the creations of 'original Indians', and have nothing to do with migrants? British colonizers used racial theories such as the Aryan invasion theory as part of their 'divide and rule' policy. Are we being racist in our discomfort with the Aryan migration theory? In the vociferous rejection of this theory, there seems to be implicit suggestion that all things good in India from the Vedas to the Indus valley civilization to the discovery of zero, are purely Indian, while all things bad, from untouchability to misogyny to homosexuality, came with foreigners such as the Greeks (who were repelled by Hindu kings) or Muslims and

Europeans (who used cunning to overthrow Hindu kings). This reeks of the fear of corruption and the desire for purity. Can immigrants and invaders not be Indians?

36

Was the Harappan civilization
Vedic or Hindu?

The Harappan civilization was an urban brick city civilization that thrived across much of north-west India between 5000 and 4000 years ago on the banks of the river Indus, and the now-dry Saraswati, and their tributaries. Scholars often describe this as a civilization of 'cities without language'. This civilization lasted for about 700 years and then died out, but not entirely. Many of its motifs and ideas survived, right through Vedic times, into the great Hindu river.

The Vedic civilization thrived in the Gangetic plains 3000 years ago. Though we have little archaeological evidence such as pottery to support this, we do have a vast corpus of literature known as the Vedas containing hymns dedicated to fire, and to a whole range of celestial gods. Scholars often describe this as a civilization of 'language without cities'. The Vedas have over 500 words that are non-Indo-European. These may have come from other linguistic groups such as Dravidian, or Munda. The word 'dharma', for example, is exclusively of Indian origin, emerging around the Indus valley before the Vedic civilization moved eastwards and settled in the Gangetic plains.

Hinduism is an umbrella term for a system of faiths that emerged in the Indian subcontinent organically over the past 5000 years and accommodates a whole variety of local traditions, thanks to an overarching framework of ideas that can be traced to the Vedas. However, like a river with many tributaries, Hinduism has many sources, not just Vedic, but also Harappan.

While there is relative certainty that the Harappan civilization was not the Vedic civilization, there is increasing evidence that by the time the Vedic civilization established itself in the Gangetic plains, it was influenced by Harappan ideas and practices. These ideas include the use of complex fire altars, ritual bathing, worship of plants, and stellar asterisms (nakshatras, such as Krittika), use of bangles, and use of sindoor.

Although the Harappan cities collapsed, the ideas found in the Harappan civilization did not die out and probably served as one of the many tributaries to the river we called Indic culture. And so, plants such as pipal, symbols such as swastika and mathematical proportions such as 5:4 (one and one quarter), which have been traced back to Harappan cities, are still very much part of contemporary Indian faith systems.

Everyone rejects the colonial theory that the Vedic civilization was created by Aryan (Indo-European) tribal invaders who destroyed the Harappan civilization. However, the relationship between the Harappan and the Vedic civilizations has divided people. One group – led by Hindu supremacists – insists that the two are the same, and they thrived in India 5000 years ago. The other group – led by Marxists – insists the two are different, and that the Harappan civilization is indigenous, but pre-Hindu, while the Vedic civilization was alien and it established itself in the Gangetic plains 3000 years ago, enslaving the descendants of Harappan cities, and 'original' tribal inhabitants of India, eventually imposing Brahminical supremacy and caste hierarchy on local people.

Scholars who do not cling to any ideology shun such extreme opinions. Among them, there seems to be a general consensus that a proto-Indo-European language/people entered India 3500 years ago via Iran from Eurasia, and mingled with the local population, which included people who still followed some beliefs and practices of the Harappan civilization, as well other tribes. This gave rise to the Vedic civilization!

So yes, the urban Harappan civilization that knew no horses and the nomadic Vedic civilization that was obsessed with horses are different, separated by time. But no, the Vedic civilization was not alien; it was shaped by many local ideas and not just Indo-European ones. Hinduism today incorporates many more ideas, besides Harappan and Vedic. Other sources are Greek, Hun, Gujjar, Chinese, Central Asian, Arabic and also European. Over time, there were separations and amalgamations of various ideas, various schools of thought that came and went.

Even today we can link modern Vedantic traditions to fire-based, masculine monastic ideals of Vedic scriptures, and modern Tantrik traditions to water-based, feminine fertility ideals of Harappan cities.

37

When did the events of the Ramayana and the Mahabharata actually occur?

There are essentially two kinds of answers: a faith-based answer, and a fact-based answer. The faith-based answer accepts what is transmitted in texts and by teachers as the complete truth, without any acute analysis. The fact-based answer is limited by the accessibility to evidence. Eventually, it all depends on what answer you are prepared to receive for the answer is complicated and mired in politics.

For example, there is archaeological evidence of cities, now submerged under the sea, near Dwarka, in Gujarat. These are probably over 4000 years old, dated to Harappan times. This is an established fact. However, the faith-based answer will tempt one to conclude that this is the island-city of Dwarka whose destruction is described in the epic the Mahabharata, the earliest available retelling of which is less than 2500 years old. The fact-based answer will say there is not enough evidence linking the two.

Hindus believe that time is cyclical. So, there is no one Ramayana or Mahabharata. These events recur in every cycle (kalpa). Each cycle has four phases (yuga) – the Ramayana takes place in the second, and the Mahabharata in the third cycle. Between each cycle there is Pralaya (end of the world) when all matter is destroyed and the only memory that survives is the Vedas.

The faith-based school believes that the ice age marked the last Pralaya. Based on astronomical information such as the position of constellations and the time of eclipses available in scriptures, they have concluded that the events in the Ramayana took place 7000 years ago and the events in the Mahabharata took place 5000 years ago. The sages Valmiki and Vyasa witnessed these events, and composed epics, which is why the two epics are called itihasa (thus it truly happened, as it was witnessed by the composers), as against puranas (old stories, heard by composers from earlier generations). The aim of the epics was not merely to share the stories of Ram and Krishna, but to reveal how they used Vedic wisdom to engage with society.

However, this traditional view is not accepted by scientists.

According to scientists, after the ice age, we find human civilization flourishing around the world, especially in river valleys. We find settlements in South Asia as confirmed by cave paintings and various Stone Age artefacts. The Harappan city civilization thrived around the rivers Indus and Saraswati in the north-west for 1000 years from 5000 years ago to 4000 years ago, with trade links to Egypt and Mesopotamia. Climate changes, and the drying of the Saraswati, led to the collapse of this civilization. We don't know what language was spoken here so we don't know if they were aware of Ram or Krishna. The only image recognizable is one that suggests Shiva in meditation, and Shakti associated with plants. But even that can be challenged.

As the Harappan civilization (cities without language) waned, the Vedic civilization (language without cities) waxed. It was marked by hymns in a language like that of a nomadic people who migrated 5000 years ago from Eurasia towards Europe in the West and India via Iran in the East. The migration of a people and/or language took place over several centuries, and they mingled with the local population, people who were descendants of Harappan cities, as well as forest-dwelling tribes. It was never an invasion as British orientalists imagined.

The events in the Mahabharata take place in the upper Gangetic plains (Indraprastha, near modern Delhi) and the behaviour of people is rather crude as compared to the very refined behaviour found in the Ramayana, which describes events occurring in the lower Gangetic plains (Ayodhya, Mithila) and further south. Can we then say that the events in the Ramayana took place after the Mahabharata, and the refinement indicates the passage of time and evolution of culture? However, this goes against what the epics themselves say. In the Mahabharata, the Pandavas are told the story of an ancient king called Ram, which makes the Ramayana, at least narratively, an earlier tale. This makes things confusing.

According to language experts, while proto-Sanskrit may have come from Eurasia, the language we call Vedic Sanskrit today emerged in the region where the Harappan cities once thrived. The people speaking Vedic Sanskrit eventually spread further east towards the Ganga where they established a thriving civilization 3000 years ago. The hymns refer to an eastward migration. References to iron are found in later hymns. Archaeologists have found painted greyware pottery in the Gangetic plains that can be dated to this period. So, we are confident that the Vedic civilization thrived in Gangetic plains 3000 years ago.

Nowadays Vedic hymns are written in a Sanskrit called Vedic Sanskrit while the oldest Ramayana and Mahabharata texts we have are written in a Sanskrit called Classical Sanskrit. The latter uses a grammar first documented by Panini who lived 2500 years ago. So, the oldest versions of the Ramayana and the Mahabharata that we have today are from less than 2500 years ago, but they could be describing events that occurred many hundred years before that.

The Mauryan kings introduced writing to India 2300 years ago and Vedic hymns started being put down in writing less than 2000 years ago. Until then the corpus of Vedic knowledge was transmitted orally. This gave the Brahmins, carriers of Vedic knowledge, special status in society. Brahmins were challenged by hermits (shramana) who valued contemplation and meditation more than rituals. They spoke words of wisdom that appealed to society. The most popular hermit was the Buddha who lived 2500 years ago. The hermits rejected Vedic rituals and the householder's life.

The Ramayana and the Mahabharata seem to have been composed as a reaction to this hermit revolution, so after the age of the Buddha, as they argue in favour of the householder's life and reveal how the hermit's wisdom can be used within the household. The story is perhaps 3000 years old, but it became a vehicle for the Vedic householder's (sansarik) values much later.

Scholars believe many Brahmins contributed to the many editions of the two epics. They were editors who were convinced that Vyasa and Valmiki composed the original tales after witnessing them. The editing took place over 600 years from 2300 years ago to 1700 years ago. In other words, the epic we have now is seen as the work of multiple, not a single, authors. Regional versions came much later: the Tamil Ramayana is about 1000 years old, the Hindi Ramayana and Mahabharata about 500 years.

Several books claiming to be the original Sanskrit Valmiki Ramayana and Vyasa Mahabharata were gathered in the nineteenth century from across India. In the twentieth century, scholars put together a 'critical' edition of what could probably be the oldest hymns. Thus, we have the critical edition of the Valmiki Ramayana by the Maharaja Sayaji Rao University Oriental Institute, Baroda, and the critical edition of the Vyasa Mahabharata by Bhandarkar Oriental Research Institute, Pune.

We can be fairly confident that the two epics reached their final narrative form 2000 years ago, and that they are possibly based on events that occurred 3000 years ago. But since many events can be found only in later texts, in regional languages, and even in Jain and Buddhist retellings, one is not entirely sure, which event is historical and which is fantasy. Dating the events before this time frame is purely a matter of faith.

Faith: 40 Insights into Hinduism

38

Were Hindus always casteist?

The word caste is a European word for clan that is used for the Indian system of jati. The word jati, in turn, is confused with the Vedic system of varna. The Vedas speak of a theoretical four-fold structure (chatur-varna). In reality, India has thousands of jatis that are crudely mapped to these four varnas, leading to much chaos and confusion. There is further confusion on the issue by equating caste with class, or caste with race, or caste with tribes.

The Vedic reference to varna is probably not physical. It is metaphorical, referring to the theoretical nature of human society. Every society in the world has divine mediums (Brahmin), landowners (Kshatriya), product producers and merchants (Vaishya) and service-providers (Shudra). In reality, Vedic society, 3000 years ago, had common people (vish) ruled by chariot-riding warriors (rajanya) who depended on mantra-chanting divine mediums (kavi or rishi).

Brahmana texts say that a man is born 'Shudra' until he is initiated into reading the Vedas after which he becomes 'Brahmin', revealing that 'Brahmin' was a position to be attained through education and contemplation, not a condition one was born into.

The process of casteism as we know it today, with strict rules of purity prohibiting inter-caste marriage, started 1900 years ago, became common 1500 years ago and rigid 1000 years ago. We know this because of recent genetic studies.

It was the British who claimed that Hindus are essentially casteist. That the idea comes from a verse in the Rig Veda that describes society as an organism made of four groups (chatur-varna) of people. They argued that 'white' Aryans invaded India and turned 'black' Dravidians into slaves who were located at the bottom of this four-fold hierarchy. Their argument was based on the translation that 'varna' means colour. It was they who tried to give every Hindu a jati, and fit the jati into the four-fold Vedic varna system, while conducting census about 100 years ago.

This colonial theory has been disproved based on genetic studies. All we known is that a linguistic group who spoke proto-Sanskrit entered India 3500 years ago and mingled extensively with the rest of the population; there was no endogamy. We also know that Hinduism is not 'commandment' based, and so scriptures merely reflect (smriti) on social reality, they do not inform it as in Islam, Christianity and Judaism.

Like all societies, Hindu society also had many communities that were located in an economic and political hierarchy. All jatis mapped themselves to the theoretical four-fold varna model. The Veda-controlling and temple-controlling jatis were seen as Brahmins who had access to divinity and so had spiritual power. The land-owning jatis were seen as Kshatriyas and so had political power. The market-controlling jatis were grouped as Vaishyas and they had economic power. The service-providing Shudras had neither spiritual, political or economic power. They were servants of all, like serfs in other feudal societies.

Following the coming of the Buddha, 2500 years ago, we find writings that refer to many communities (jati) that followed a single vocation. There is reference to guilds of potters, weavers, metal smiths. They secured their knowledge systems by preventing inter-jati marriages. However, this was not a strict rule. In Buddhist literature, we find two divergent ideas. One that karma determines the kind of jati we are born into: those that dominate or those that serve. As per Jataka tales, the good karma of past lives enables Siddhartha Gautama to become Buddha. However, we also hear Buddha stating (something that is repeated in the Mahabharata as well) that a true 'Brahmin' is determined by deeds not birth. Thus, we see tension between the birth-doctrine and the deed-doctrine in matters related to jati and varna.

In Jain stories, we hear how the Tirthankara's embryo is transferred from the womb of a Brahmin woman into the womb of Kshatriya woman. So, Jains, who were monastic, also recognized a society made of multiple communities. In Hindu epics, we find stories where men are denied choice. Karna is mocked for wanting to learn archery as his foster father is a charioteer. Shambuka is beheaded by Ram for abandoning his trade and becoming an ascetic. Krishna tells Arjuna that his duty is to perform his role as determined by his family. The Bhagavad Gita seems anti-monastic with Arjuna being told not to give up the world as monks do but to do his duty as a warrior and member of royal family. Note: the only choice here is to either to follow the family vocation or become a monk. You could not really choose a vocation, as per Hindu, Jain or Buddhist lore. Your vocation comes from the father.

In many of these stories, we hear of a 'chandala' who lives in crematoriums, is surrounded by dogs, and generally shunned by people. Who are these people? The 'lower' castes? Shiva is often depicted as a god who lives with dogs in crematoriums, who is feared and shunned by 'Brahmin' leaders like Daksha. Daksha is obsessed with purity and Shiva mocks ideas of purity. Is this the clash of ancient Hindu 'conservatives' and Hindu 'liberals'?

With the rise of Puranic literature, something changes. This is roughly 1500 years ago, when temples are being built; Buddhism is on the wane; Tantrik Hinduism which values the body, is on the rise; and the dharma-shastras, including the Manusmriti, are guiding principles. All of society is based on jati-system. Every individual belongs to a community (jati). Earlier, marriage within one's jati was preferred, but it was not obligatory. From this period onwards, as genetic studies show, the rules became increasingly rigid and draconian. Then came the doctrine of purity (shuddhi).

Faith: 40 Insights into Hinduism

Some communities were labelled 'impure'. In the last 1000 years, villages and cities were designed so that the purest, not necessarily the wealthiest or the most powerful, stayed in the centre next to the temple, which was the pure navel of the settlement. Those who were less pure stayed at a distance. And the least pure stayed at the margins. And the tribal communities, stayed in the forest. The people who lived in the margins were 'ritually unclean' owing to their profession, which involved dealing with dead bodies and excrement. It all sounds highly logical: but it dehumanized people, denied them human dignity, and access to common resources like water and education. Who set up these cities? In all probability Brahmins who were given this power by kings. Thus, we have many copper inscriptions in Odisha, the Deccan and Tamil Nadu, in the past 1500 years, detailing land grants to Brahmins who set up new villages (brahmadeya settlements), and created an administrative structure to collect grain-tax on behalf of the king.

Adi Shankara, who lived in the eighth century, once met a Chandala and asked him to step aside. The Chandala argued, 'You want my impure body to move or the pure soul?' This story has been interpreted in many ways and shows the gap between idealistic Hinduism where knowledge of soul (atma) helps us rise above caste hierarchy and practical Hinduism where caste hierarchy thrives. Around the same time lived Nandanar, a Tamil Shiva-saint (nayamnar), who was denied entry into the Shiva temple at Chidambaram. Some claim he passed through fire and turned into a Brahmin and only then was allowed entry, thus reaffirming the idea of keeping impure people away from the temple.

In twelfth-century Karnataka, we hear of Basava challenging the caste system and being thrown out of his job in the king's court for encouraging inter-caste marriage. In fourteenth-century Maharashtra, we hear of Chokhamela who was not allowed to enter the temple of Vitthala in Pandharpur, and so his shrine was built on the temple steps where it still stands. Marathi poet-saints like Dyaneshwara and Tukaram and Eknath were also persecuted for writing about God in local languages, rather than Sanskrit, and for promoting the idea of equality before God. Similar songs of equality were sun by Ravidas, whose verses are found in the Granth Sahib of Sikhs, a religion that emerged from the rejection of the caste system.

In the sixteenth century, there were five poet-saints (pancha-sakha) in Odisha who identify themselves as servant-sages (Shudra-muni) and wrote poems about Krishna in Odia, challenging the might of the Brahmins who controlled the temple, and restricted their access to the temple. Even today at the gateway of the Puri temple, there is another image of Jagannath meant for 'lower' castes, who were not allowed to enter the temple. Around the same time, in Udupi Karnataka, Kanaka was not allowed to enter the temple. So, he sang songs from behind the temple and we are told the east-facing image turned to face the west and the wall breached so that Kanaka could see the lord (darshan).

Faith: 40 Insights into Hinduism

Until 100 years ago, in many villages of India, there were some communities that were not just allowed to use the village well, they had to wear a broom to wipe away their footprints, carry a pot to spit in so that it did not fall on the ground and contaminate it, and a drum to announce their arrival. All this because their family vocation as per the jati system was to clean toilets and deal with animal carcasses. In other words, they could not change their vocation, and at the same time were deprived of dignity for it as they were considered impure by birth.

The idea of purity is what established casteism in India. Purity has been manipulated by many Hindus to create a draconian hierarchy, despite opposition from other Hindus, especially the poet-sages. Academician-activists tend to focus on the former as 'real' Hindus and ignore the latter. They ignore the idea that notions of purity and impurity pervade all human society in various forms, from taboos in ancient tribes to fascism in modern times.

The cancer of casteism in India began with the rise of the doctrine of purity 2000 years ago. Now this doctrine of purity is spreading around the world. It takes the form of discrimination and a yearning for a pure 'homogenous' paradise with no diversity. You see this in the speeches of politicians who want to exclude everyone except those who subscribe to their party politics. This is neo-casteism.

The 'visa' system of nation states was designed to keep out poor and unskilled people from 'developed' countries, hence the rage against immigrants. People argue that when immigrants come, they 'pollute' the value system of the land. For example, many Muslim immigrants reject the idea that women and homosexuals have rights. Likewise, in India, non-violent Jain communities use their political power to protect themselves from the 'pollution' of meat eaters. Muslims in Pakistan and Iran reject the 'pollution' of liberal values, including Sufism, that is seen as idolatry (shirk). Marxists see capitalism as pollution; Maoists see development as pollution; Dalits of India are being told Hinduism is pollution and Buddhism is purity; vegetarians insist that meat-eaters are impure; heterosexuals insist homosexuals are impure; monogamists are convinced polyamorists are impure.

The idea that Hindus are essentially casteist, that Brahmins, through the 'commandments' of the Manusmriti, created this system from the top is a very simplistic understanding of a system that is even followed by 'lower' castes and Muslims and Christians who even today are highly selective about who their son or daughter should marry. Reformers argue oppressed people who follow casteism suffer from Stockholm Syndrome and reject the idea that they are using their own agency and thus support the system. Equally simplistic is the idea that positive discrimination and reservation system will create a fairer society. In fact, it creates a passionate backlash and a further strengthening of boundaries between castes, with new four-fold systems being created such as scheduled tribes, scheduled castes, other backward castes and general category. Some people believe in the 'trickle down' effect; others believe in an 'instant revolution'. Neither really works. So, the situation remains complicated and unstable with no simple answer, but a lot of self-righteous rage on every side.

39

Did the arrival of Muslim invaders 1000 years ago destroy Hindu culture?

Historians avoid the term Islamic invasions and prefer using words like Arab, Turk and Mongol/Mughal invasions for two reasons. First, many see these invasions are motivated by economics and politics, not religion. Second, they want to avoid the communal vocabulary. Many Hindus feel the very same historians do not give Hinduism the same respect. They argue that if you do not link the spread of Islam to violence, how can you link Hinduism to casteism? Why can't both be seen as outcomes of politics and economics, not religion?

Invasions, like droughts and epidemics, result in migration and shifts in population and the recalibration of culture. There is transplantation and transformation of ideas. And so, Americans today practice yoga, not realizing its Indian (or should we say Hindu) roots and Indians drink coffee not realizing its Arabic (or should we say Muslim) roots.

The Indian subcontinent is relatively isolated from the rest of the world because of the Himalayas bordering the north and the sea bordering the south. Still, people have come through mountain passes and seaports for over 5000 years. Some came to trade, some came to loot, some came to rule and some came looking for a better home. Each one changed India. This means India has always had foreign influence over its history in various degrees – from Egyptians, Persians, Arabs, Chinese, Greeks, Romans, Central Asians and Europeans.

The arrival of Muslim invaders 1000 years ago dramatically transformed Hindu culture. Like in any invasion, there was destruction and trauma. However, the damage was neither absolute nor permanent. Over time, Hindu culture recovered and adapted to the new realities and eventually a new Hindu culture emerged that engaged with Islam both philosophically and socially.

Indian culture is like a masala box. The dominant spices are identified as Hindu, but not all of them came into being here, or at the same time. Some came into being following indigenous challenges, such as the rise of Buddhism, which introduced ideas of monastic orders. Others came into being following foreign challenges, such as the arrival of the Greeks who introduced the idea of stone temples enshrining stone images of heroes and gods, very different from the portable imageless rituals of Vedic culture, or the river and mountain and tree gods of local tribes. Some spices refuse to be identified

as Hindu, but do not mind being called Indian. Sor
insist on being identified as non-Indian. Then there
that are best called global, as they are found everywhere.

As in any culture, there are many Indians and Hindus who
believe in the idea of 'pure' culture. Notions of 'purity' are
always mythological (subjective), never scientific (objective),
however they play a key role in shaping culture. This becomes
evident when one thinks about the influence of the Portuguese
on India. The Portuguese brought potato to India from South
America; they also spread Christianity. Many purists don't see
the potato as a foreign vegetable. But they do see Christianity
as a foreign idea, and hate it vehemently, even as they eat
aloo parathas.

Islam rose 1400 years ago in Arabia. Islam reached Kerala
via sea traders during the lifetime of the Prophet Muhammad.
When we speak of an Islamic invasion, we usually refer to
the invasion of north India (Punjab and Gangetic plain)
that eventually impacted the east (Bengal) and then the rest
of the subcontinent. This happened in two phases: the first,
less successful one spearheaded by Arabs that reached the
borders of India nearly 1200 years ago, and the second, more
successful one spearheaded by Turks and Mongols that began
800 years ago.

In the first phase of the Islamic invasion, most of India
remained unaffected. The spread of Islam destroyed the
Buddhist and Zoroastrian centres that once thrived along the
Silk Road. If there was any impact on Indian thought, it was
indirect, not direct. Some people say that although bhakti and

monotheism are alluded to in the 2000-year-old Bhagavad Gita, the widespread popularity of these ideas in the last 1000 years may have been the result of Islamic influence.

The second phase of Islamic invasion saw great violence. Warlords from Afghanistan and Central Asia such as the Ghaznavids sought to loot the legendary wealth of India, mostly hoarded in temples. Fuel for these raids was provided by the religious zeal to wipe out the land of idolaters. These invaders wiped out cities and temples in their wake, and went back with gold and slaves. We can argue endlessly on how much damage was physical, and how much was psychological, how much was real and how much was propaganda, how much was motivated by economics, and how much by religious zeal, but the fact is, Hinduism was never the same.

Over time, many Turk, Afghan and Mongol warlords decided to settle in India. From around 800 years ago, a sultanate rose in Delhi led by Mamluks, Khiljis, Lodis and Tughlaqs. Around 600 years ago, there rose sultanates in the Bengal and Deccan regions. From around 400 years ago, the Mughal Empire was established in north India, and gradually spread to the south. Temples in places such as Madurai in the south, Ujjain in central India, Puri in the east, Somnath in the west, retained the memory of the plunder by Muslim kings in local lore.

But in these times, dramatic changes took place in Hinduism. Some happened because of Islam. Others despite it. According to one theory, Islam in India acquired a unique Indian flavour. Only here did Islam co-exist with another religion in harmony. In Europe, it fought bitter wars with Christianity. In South East Asia, Buddhism and Hinduism were seen as foundational cultural influences but with Islam clearly as the religion on top. In India, Islam became the practice of certain castes. For example, there could be 'high-caste' landowners who were also Muslim. Or there were 'low-caste' butchers who also happened to be Muslim. This created a kind of tension-filled harmony with violence on the edges but no full-fledged communal conflict.

It is during the last 1000 years that acharyas such as Ramanuja, Madhva, Vallabha, Nimbarka and Chaitanya consolidated theistic Vedanta philosophy that is considered by many as the main foundation of Hinduism today.

It is also within the last 1000 years that we find the rise of various sacred Hindu literatures in regional languages including most of the Ramayanas and the Mahabharatas that we find in Tamil, Telugu, Malayalam, Kannada, Assamese, Odia, Bengali, Gujarati, Marathi, Marwari and Hindi.

While many temples in places such as Kashmir, Gujarat and the Gangetic plains were destroyed and their pillars used to build mosques, many new grand temples were built at ancient sites by local Hindu kings in the last 1000 years to show their power. The current edifice of the Jagannath temple that we see today was built 800 years ago by Chodagangadeva. Again, most of the grand structures we see in Tamil Nadu and Andhra Pradesh such as the Meenakshi temple in Madurai are about 400 years old, built by Nayaka kings. In the north, people avoided building temples, and chose to worship the deity inside homes, giving rise to the Thakur-ghar or Haveli culture seen in Rajasthan and central India.

Bhakti songs of Meera, Ravidas, Tukaram, Annamaya, Kshetrayya, and Purandaradasa were all written in the past 500 years. While the oral tradition has been the mainstay of Hinduism, in many Hindu communities, manuscripts of the Bhagavata or the Ramayana started being enshrined and worshipped, such as in the Bhagavata-ghara in Odisha, which indicates the increasingly popular value given to books, clearly an Islamic influence.

In the last 400 years, the sultans of the Deccan patronized Hindustani classical music, the nawabs of Oudh celebrated Krishna-leela and Ram-leela and established the Bada Mangal festival of Hanuman in Lucknow. Holi became a royal festival, celebrated by Hindu and Muslim kings. The Mughal court patronized Persian painters who established the Indian miniature style of painting that resulted in fine art works for various local Rajput kings and Hindu noblemen on themes from the Ramayana, Mahabharata, Gita Govinda, Bhagavata and Puranas. These are displayed in museums around the world.

Villages were organized along caste lines before the arrival of Islam and the system continued even after. Those who converted to Islam continued to follow their family vocation and retain their caste.

There were many communities where the lines between Hinduism and Islam were not rigid. For example, many Rajasthani musicians who sang Hindu bardic lore were Muslim. In Bengal, patua artists who painted the epics on long pieces of paper were Muslims. In Kerala, there is the Mapilla the Ramayana of the Malabari Muslims, where we find words like sharia used in the Ramayana. The famous ballad 'Padmavat' about the attack on Chittor by Allauddin Khilji was composed by a Muslim poet, Malik Muhammad Jayasi. In many shrines, holy men were seen as pirs by Muslims and as jogis by Hindus. Many Muslim kings had Hindu courtiers (Mansingh in the court of Akbar) and many Hindu kings had Muslim courtiers (Hakin Khan Sur who fought alongside Rana Pratap in Haldighati).

Costumes changed. In north India, the ghunghat, or the garment covering women's heads and faces became common in Hindu households, a practice still not seen in the south. In the temples of Shrinathji in Nathdvara one of the many attires of the deity was Mughal-vesha. In Srirangam, the deity was given a Muslim consort, Tuluka Nachiyar. In many parts of the south, the deities had Muslim guards and Muslim companions such as Vavar of Ayyappa-swami and Mutthala Ravuttan of Draupadi-Amman.

It was the British who preferred to see India as a collection of religions rather than a collection of castes. They defined Hinduism and made it a collection of castes, excluding those who followed Abrahamic religions, village reality notwithstanding. It was the British who tried to force-fit 3000 jatis of India into the four varnas of the Vedas. Caste politics meant no jati had majority anywhere in India, and was too complicated to handle. Religion politics meant Indians could very easily be distracted by communal politics.

Independent India tried to suppress (or exploit) caste and religious politics, but could not escape language politics. Now, we are faced with caste, religious and language politics, that often distract us from the economic woes of the land. Even if there was no Islam, Indians would still have to face the issues of caste and language and even gender politics. History, politics, economics, culture and religion are very complex subjects.

When people try to reduce Indian history by speaking of 1000 years of Muslim slavery (or for that matter, Brahmanical hegemony, or men's enslavement of women, or how heterosexuals have rendered queer people invisible, or white people control the world, or that Han Chinese control the Orient), one must always remember that the world and its history cannot be explained so simply. Be aware of the controlling nature of these half-truths. Partial truths are far more dangerous than falsehoods.

40

Is the samosa Indian, or Vedic?

The samosa originated in the Middle East and came to India following the arrival of Central Asian Muslim kings into the subcontinent roughly 800 years ago. Was it shaped after Egyptian pyramids? We can only speculate. It was called 'samba' or 'sambosa', and the filling was meat. The earliest reference to it is found 1000 years ago in Persian literature. Amir Khusro and Ibn Batuta refer to 'samushak' or 'sanbusa' being served 600 years ago in the royal palaces of the Delhi Sultanate.

However, today, for most people, samosa has a potato filling. This was probably an Indian innovation. Interestingly, the potato is not an Indian vegetable either. The Portuguese brought it to India from South America about 400 years ago. Today, we cannot imagine an Indian dish without potatoes, but this is a recent addition to our diet, just like chillies.

We have embraced it so wholeheartedly that we cannot believe it is of foreign origin.

Many ancient Hindu temples have kitchens but few include potato or chillies in the cuisine. Instead they use pumpkin or gourd instead of potato, and long green pepper instead of chillies. This suggests the foreign origin of potato and chillies. This is similar to the practice in many Hindu temples of not using rose petals for worship of the main deity, as roses are said to have come with the Mughals. However, over time, when people forget their foreign origin, these vegetables, spices and flowers come to be included in rituals, and are seen as Indian, worthy of being offered to Hindu gods. Thus, it is not uncommon nowadays to see deities enshrined in temples adorned with rose petals and the offering including puri-bhaji, with the bhaji containing potatoes. Chillies are an integral part of Goddess worship nowadays and of rituals designed to ward off the evil eye.

The words 'yava' and 'dhana' in the Rig Veda probably refer to barley that was used to make cakes and pancakes that were part of the yagna ceremony. Some have speculated that the word 'paratha' probably has a Vedic origin, from puro-dasha? Did Indians have dishes similar to the samosa with vegetable or meat fillings, but in pancake form? We can only speculate.

While India received ingredients and dishes from other lands, it also gave ingredients and dishes to other lands. Sugarcane, for example, spread from South Asia to other parts of the world. Jaggery reached Europe during the Roman era as medicine mixed in ghee, not as food. Sugar as we know it reached

Europe about 1000 years ago. Before that, the main sweetener in meals was honey. Indians, however, took jaggery for granted. And what is now called Chai-tea in Europe and America came from India. The idea of brewing tea in milk is about 100 years old and originated in Indian dhabas. Using milk for brewing tea would horrify the traditional Chinese who invented tea drinking after an emperor insisted that everyone drink boiled water for health reasons.

I would end by saying that the current samosa, with its potato filling (or peas filling, for Jains who shun root vegetables), is an Indian creation based on several inputs from Central Asians, Persians and the Portuguese. Like Hinduism, it is very much a combination of various spiritual tributaries. For the hardliners, who feel Hinduism must be Vedic, we can call it Vedic, in the sense of being all-encompassing, for everything, ultimately, originates from the primal purusha.